OUTREACH
TEAMS
THAT WIN

G·R·O·W

JERRY N. TIDWELL

LifeWay Press®
Nashville, Tennessee

No part of this book may be reproduced or transmitted in any form or by any
means, electronic or mechanical, including photocopying and recording, or by any
information storage or retrieval system, except as may be expressly permitted in
writing by the publisher. Requests for permission should be addressed in writing to:
LifeWay Press ®; One LifeWay Plaza; Nashville, TN 37234-0175.

ISBN 0-7673-9276-0

This book is a resource in the Pastoral Ministries category
of the Christian Growth Study Plan.
Course LS-0068 and LS-0082

Dewey Decimal Classification: 269
Subject Heading: EVANGELISTIC WORK

Unless otherwise noted, all Scripture quotations are from
the King James Version of the Bible.
Scripture quotations identified NKJV are from the New King James Version.
Copyright © 1979, 1980, 1982, Thomas Nelson, Inc. Publishers.
Used by permission.

Printed in the United State of America

Leadership and Adult Publishing
One LifeWay Plaza
Nashville, Tennessee 37234-0175

Dedication

This book is dedicated to the memory of my friend
Robert W. (Bob) Brian. Bob left this world while doing
what he loved best—leading others in preparation
for praise and worship of our Lord Jesus Christ
at West Jackson Baptist Church, Jackson, Tennessee.

Contents

Foreword

Pastors and people, teachers and deacons, members and worshiping families will be encouraged beyond compare by this book on ministers and church growth written by Dr. Jerry Tidwell. It is not a volume of mere speculation; but it has been created and written by a man of God who has experienced every detail of the fortunes, good and bad, of those who pour their lives into the building of a great lighthouse for Jesus.

This whole world desperately needs this book on outreach ministries. Up and down every street in every city are those who are lost, families and friends and neighbors and acquaintances and fellow citizens in the communities where we ourselves are rearing our children and building our families. God Himself knew of our desperate need insomuch that He sent His only begotten Son to teach us the way of life, to die for our sins according to the Scripture, and to go before us in the evangelization of our families, of our communities, of our cities and nation, and of our whole world. Fortunate and blessed is the man of God in the pulpit who is true to this sacred vision of our Savior, and fortunate and blessed is the church that follows the leadership of that consecrated and dedicated pastor.

Get this book. Read and pray over every word. Share it with the members and with the organizations of the house of God. Pour your lives into that outreach ministry. You yourselves will be the first to be astonished at the heavenly reward and the blessings of the Lord God upon you.

W.A. Criswell, pastor emeritus
First Baptist Church, Dallas, Texas

Acknowledgments

I would like to thank the many pioneers, pastors, and professors who encouraged me in the area of church growth and evangelism. The previous works of W. A. Criswell, Andy Anderson, Peter Wagner, Ralph Neighbor, and Ron Lewis have contributed greatly to this project. Also, special thanks to F. B. Huey, Roy Fish, and James Eaves whose work at Southwestern Baptist Theological Seminary gave me knowledge and tools necessary for church growth and personal evangelism.

Introduction

After a demanding Monday filled with a funeral, hospital visits, and staff meetings, I was happy to sit down about 9:00 p.m. for a visit with my little girl, Chrissy. Just before her third rendition of the "Barney Song," the phone rang.

I'm not sure how other pastors feel, but Mondays really don't excite me about ministry. I'm usually recovering from preaching 3 messages, attending 144 meetings (maybe it's only 4, but it feels like 144), and listening to 5 people complain that the American flag and the Christian flag are on the wrong sides of the platform.

Monday is supposed to be the day when pastors can be human—you know, yell at the cat and kick the dog. My darling wife, Kathy, and my little girl work hard to make Monday a great day for me. And talking on the phone for a half hour is not an exciting thought.

Kathy answered the call and said with a smile, "It's for you!" The man at the other end of the line was Bruce Williams.

Bruce had called to ask me to pray for him about an operation he was having to correct an aneurysm in his brain. This was not an unusual request, except that I had no idea who Bruce Williams was!

After I prayed with him, he asked, "Could I talk with someone about getting my life in order?"

I said, "Sure," and took down his address.

Since the next evening was our scheduled outreach night, I assigned this visit to someone who could effectively share his faith. During the report time the visitor enthusiastically reported that Bruce and his 11-year-old son prayed to receive Christ. Because of the serious nature of the surgery that was to take place that same week, several of the G•R•O•W team members followed up on this family. I personally thought that this was one of those decisions made as a

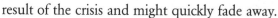

Could it be that many persons miss the chance to see lives changed because their church does not have an ongoing, aggressive outreach ministry?

result of the crisis and might quickly fade away.

Before Bruce and his son could make public professions of their faith, the surgery took place. Bruce had complications. The surgery led to heart failure that almost claimed his life. After doctors worked to help him recover from the heart problem, Bruce suffered a stroke that left him paralyzed on one side of his body. The damage from the stroke forced him to spend several weeks in painful rehabilitation in the hospital. It was a difficult ordeal, especially for a man in his early 40s.

Most people either had forgotten about Bruce's decision for Christ or doubted his chances of ever making it to a worship service. Then one Sunday it happened! Without any prior indication, Bruce had slipped into the service. When the invitation was extended, he shuffled down the aisle with his cane and his 11-year-old son. He and his son publicly confessed their faith in Christ. Both were baptized and are active in church today.

I often have reflected on the circumstances surrounding Bruce's decision for Christ. If our church had not had an aggressive, organized, outreach program, I may have become occupied with other ministry needs and never made it to share Christ with Bruce Williams. Could it be that many persons miss the chance to see lives changed because their church does not have an ongoing, aggressive outreach ministry?

This book is designed to encourage believers in evangelism and outreach. It will, however, go beyond encouragement. It will provide principles and practical ideas for developing and implementing an effective outreach program in your church.

Recent trends in church growth dictate that we define our foundational philosophy of growth before tabulating our success. While

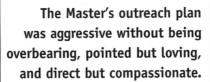

The Master's outreach plan was aggressive without being overbearing, pointed but loving, and direct but compassionate.

demographics and marketing trends are beneficial tools for those who promote church-growth strategies, these tools should not be used as catalysts for starting a new church or as a strategy of outreach in an existing church. Should a church form around a sociological trend? Should our growth philosophy focus on one common emotional need? What should be the basis of the church-growth strategies in our local churches? The foundation of this book focuses on three basic presuppositions as the basis for outreach:

1. People's need for God.
2. God's desire to have fellowship with people.
3. The Master's own plan of evangelism and outreach.

The Master's outreach plan was aggressive without being overbearing, pointed but loving, and direct but compassionate. His plan was well organized but not boring, filled with creativity but uncompromising. The outreach plan covered in this book needs to be studied, prayed over, and implemented by every local church. The principles of this practical program are not new, but they hold a new freshness for those who will digest them.

My thanks go to the fine members of Grace Baptist Church in Tullahoma, Tennessee, and West Jackson Baptist Church in Jackson, Tennessee. They have faithfully carried out the G•R•O•W outreach program with great success.

These churches are unique, yet both experienced exciting growth when this program was implemented. When I began as pastor of Grace Baptist Church, the congregation was averaging just over 60 people in Sunday School. Three years later the congregation was consistently having more than four hundred in Sunday School. We did not have any great, one-time surges in attendance. We experienced growth week by week and month by month over a three-year period.

> **When people are motivated, mobilized, and focused on the biblical principles of evangelism and outreach, they become empowered by God's Spirit.**

The only similarities between Grace Church and West Jackson Church are that both were suffering from low morale and were declining when I was called to the church. Grace was informal and nontraditional; West Jackson was a time-honored, traditional 2,400-member church. Because of its location in a transitional, residential neighborhood, it had been slowly declining for 15 years. In just over two years after the G•R•O•W program was implemented at West Jackson, the attendance climbed from an average of 480 in Sunday School to 840 in the spring of 1997. The church voted to relocate to a 50-acre campus in the northern part of Jackson, Tennessee.

When people are motivated, mobilized, and focused on the biblical principles of evangelism and outreach, they become empowered by God's Spirit. Lives are changed, and churches grow.

I arrived at the G•R•O•W principles developed in this book in an unusual way. Like many pastors, I was discouraged about the complacency and apathy that seemed to permeate my congregations and others like them. I had been a high-school football coach in Alabama before attending seminary. I began to reflect on the basic philosophies of building a winning team. The process of building a winning team involves:

- A coaching staff who will not settle for anything less than winning.
- A team that is willing to work hard.
- A strategy that the team is capable of carrying out.
- Matching players with compatible positions.
- An attitude that expects to win.

With these principles in mind, I sat down and put on paper five principles of outreach and evangelism that would help us win. The first five chapters develop these five principles.

Part I

Building a Winning Team

Chapter 1

Sowing and Reaping

The first principle that serves as a foundation to the G•R•O•W• outreach program is the principle of sowing and reaping. This is a biblically based principle. Matthew 13:54 tells us that, when Jesus entered his hometown of Nazareth, the people who lived there simply could not relate to this "hometown" boy being a miracle worker. They saw Him only as the "carpenter's son," or the "brother of James." I am convinced that Jesus really wanted to do something special for the hometown folks. But Matthew 13:57-58 records: "And they were offended in him. But Jesus said unto them, A prophet is not without honour, save in his own country, and in his own house. And he did not many mighty works there because of their unbelief."

This has to be one of the saddest verses in the Bible. The people of Nazareth missed seeing God's glory revealed through His Son because of their unbelief. They did not receive anything from Jesus because they were not expecting anything from Him. Warren Wiersbe said, "These people walked by sight and not by faith."[1]

The trouble with many of us is that we are a lot like the Nazarenes. We walk by sight instead of faith in the areas of evangelism and outreach. We miss seeing God's glory revealed through His Son because our level of expectancy is not very high. Could it be that Jesus passes through many of our churches every week with anticipation of doing many "mighty works"; but we, like the Nazarenes, do not prepare for the presence of the Savior?

That is where the "sowing and reaping" comes in. Our preparation involves sowing seeds of testimony and love in expectation of the mighty works of Jesus. The letters G•R•O•W embody this principle. God Rewards Our Work is an outgrowth of the sowing and reaping principle.

One of the things I love most about the apostle Paul is his work ethic. Paul was a stick-to-it, hard-working sort of guy. In Galatians 6:7, Paul used God's principle of sowing and reaping to illustrate to the Galatians the repercussions of sin: "Be not deceived; God is not mocked: for whatsoever a man soweth, that shall he also reap."

The "numbers" game was God's idea. God created an order by which we must plant, cultivate, and water before we reap the harvest.

Having been raised on a farm where gardens and crops were in abundance, I have always understood the reality of this principle. Sometimes seeds were planted that did not come up or produce a harvest. But one thing was for certain: If *no* seeds were planted, there would be *no* harvest. The same is true in outreach. We have been guilty of expecting a harvest where there has been no sowing or preparation.

Elmer Towns said, "The lack of growth in the contemporary Southern Baptist statistics stems from less emphasis on evangelism today than in the past."[2] For whatever reason, we have become more concerned with marketing the church than evangelizing the sinner. God will reward our work if our motives are pure and our commitment is consistent. The following chart indicates the impact of an organized outreach program on the weekly number of visitors in the worship services at West Jackson Baptist Church.

West Jackson Baptist Church (Spring 1993)		
(No Organized Outreach Program)		
Average Sunday School Attendance 480	Average Weekly Contacts less than 100	Average Number of Weekly Visitors 8
West Jackson Baptist Church (Spring 1997)		
(G•R•O•W Outreach Program in Place)		
Average Sunday School Attendance 840	Average Weekly Contacts 900	Average Number of Weekly Visitors 140

Once again, as in the case of Grace Baptist Church, mentioned in the introduction, there were no great surges of growth. There was a consistent increase over the 2½ years reflected in the data.

Church growth consultants over the past few years have suggested that it takes 13–15 contacts (intentional, personal efforts toward getting someone to church) to produce one visitor. While I am sure that is true, as surveyed by a collection of churches with and without organized outreach programs, the G•R•O•W program has experienced a better ratio of visitors. The data collected over the last five years involving this program indicated that it has taken an average of six to eight contacts to produce one visitor. Regardless of the ratio, the fact is you do not reap if you do not sow!

In 1 Corinthians 3, Paul addressed the issue of harvest. The Corinthians had difficulty with personalities; they compared "head coaches" or preachers. Even today's churches talk about pastors and

> **At the very center of everything that happens on outreach night is the report of the results from personal visitation.**

staff members as if they were the heads of sports teams rather than churches. Paul said in 1 Corinthians 3:8 that all the true laborers are "one." One plants, another waters, but God gives the increase!

Lyle Schaller has always been on the cutting edge of church growth. Yet in his book *Growing Plans*, Schaller said: "Despite this plethora of creative ideas and programs, the best single approach still is the old-fashioned system of personal visitation. This system affirms the value of face-to-face relationships and requires the pastor and lay volunteers to call, on a regular basis, on individuals and families who do not have an active relationship with any worshiping congregation."[3]

Neither Schaller nor I would suggest that personal visitation is the only effective means of outreach. After all, the G•R•O•W program itself employs several methods of outreach. But at the very center of everything that happens on outreach night is the report of the results from personal visitation. An outreach or evangelistic program cannot be successful unless the results are qualified by the biblical principle of "sowing and reaping."

---

[1] Warren W. Wiersbe, *The Bible Exposition Commentary,* vol. 1 (Wheaton, IL: Victor Books, 1989), 48.
[2] Elmer L. Towns, *The Complete Book of Church Growth* (Wheaton, IL: Tyndale House Publishers, 1981), 212.
[3] Lyle E. Schaller, *Growing Plans* (Nashville, TN: Abingdon Press, 1983), 9.

Chapter 2

Involving Every Member

When the recruitment drive began for G•R•O•W outreach at West Jackson Baptist Church, Don Smith approached me and with sincere apology shared that he did not think he would be comfortable doing personal visitation. I told him the program had other areas in which he could serve and asked him to please attend the training sessions before he made up his mind. He did, and his confidence grew. He started out by assisting with child care on Tuesday evenings and then became a part of a letter-writing team. After hearing the reports from several visit sessions, Don decided to try personal visitation. The rest is history! Don is now one of our most successful visitors and heads up our welcome ministry on Sundays. The fact is, Don Smith never would have attended a "visitation only" outreach night.

The second important principle of the G•R•O•W outreach program is that of every-member involvement. Knowing that building a winning team requires getting every player involved in some way, I knew I must find an avenue where every member of the church could feasibly be involved in the outreach program. We have used letter writing, phone calling, and crisis ministry as parts of the program. I know that some other programs use some of the same ideas. The difference is that we place extreme importance on each facet of the program. Letter writing and phone calling are not provided just to

> **The principle that we must grasp is that Jesus calls all believers to be a part of the Great Commission.**

give people something to do if they do not want to visit. The letter-writing plan is so intense and personal that we have sometimes asked some who wanted to visit to stay in and write letters. This action affirmed these areas of outreach and kept them from being perceived as token responsibilities.

Having said that, let me admit that we do see these areas as levels of entry for many people who would not ordinarily participate in a visitation-only outreach. Many of these people gain the confidence to become tremendous soul-winners.

For those who would suggest that letter writing and other responsibilities are only token in nature, let me remind them that the apostle Paul used a letter-writing campaign with better than average success. As a matter of fact, try to imagine how many times his letter to the Romans has been used to lead someone into a personal relationship with Christ.

The principle of every-member involvement is also biblical. Jesus' commission in Matthew 28:19 was given to all believers. "Go ye therefore, and teach all nations, baptizing them in the name of the Father, and of the Son, and of the Holy Ghost."

The Greek text reveals that the participle employed in "go ye therefore" may best be translated "as you are going." The principle we must grasp is that Jesus calls all believers to be a part of the Great Commission. After all, the church is the *ecclesia*—the "ones called out."

Peter must have been reassured to know that the first and last thing Jesus said to him was the same instruction. Surely the Lord Himself planned it that way. Jesus issued the first command in Matthew 4:19 when he saw Simon Peter and his brother Andrew fishing on the Sea of Galilee. Jesus said, "Follow me, and I will make you fishers of men."

Peter must have reminisced about that first moment when he heard the last words of Jesus, "Go ye therefore" in Matthew 28:19. Maybe that is why the disciples' work eventually was so successful. They had no doubt about the mission and the fact that all believers were to do their part.

We must share with our people the first, last, and all the words of Jesus in relationship to the Great Commission. When I am forced to be away from home, I always dread saying goodbye to my wife. As difficult as that is, I can assure you that the last words I say are the ones that are dearest to my heart. It may be, "I love you," "I'll miss you," or, "Don't forget to pick me up at the airport." But whatever I say, it certainly is the most pressing thought on my mind. I have a feeling the same was true with Jesus and His last words. Certainly no one could reject the emphasis Jesus placed on "every member involvement." When we attempt to implement strategies that use only a selected few, we fail to carry out Jesus' last command.

Chapter 3

Having Fun with Outreach!

This may sound a bit shallow, but I believe Jesus and the disciples had fun. Nothing can compare with what Peter, James, and John must have experienced with Jesus at the transfiguration. It was so exciting that Peter wanted to put up tents and spend the night (see Matt. 17:4).

What about the day the disciples watched five loaves and two fish multiplied when Jesus blessed the food and fed more than five thousand people? After dinner, Jesus called for a "doggy bag" to handle the leftovers. That must have been fun!

And let us not forget when Jesus' buddy Lazarus died. Jesus turned the funeral into a feast and celebration when He told Lazarus to "come forth" from the grave. The disciples must have felt like they were "hot stuff" being with Jesus.

Being a part of Jesus' outreach ministry was demanding, time-consuming, and required sacrifice; but it was also fun! The G•R•O•W program attempts to deprogram people from the guilt and negative feelings they may have acquired about visitation and outreach. The pastor and staff must communicate that "outreach is fun." Jesus motivated people in a positive way to join Him in a world-changing mission. We must motivate with words and actions regarding outreach.

I must confess that I am sometimes tempted to use the wrong methods to motivate people. For instance, when I was coaching football, I might make a statement like, "If you men work real hard today, we'll let you go home early," and it would sometimes work. The fact is, we were going to let them go home early anyway!

We ask our outreach team members to wear name tags during outreach night in order to get better acquainted with one another. After a rather low attendance one night, I threatened to wear the name tags of those absent from outreach during the morning service. Bad idea! It would have been negative reinforcement at best.

One of the ways we make outreach fun is by serving refreshments. I know a lot of churches serve a full meal for the outreach teams, but I prefer to have them eat, drink, and be merry during the outreach time itself. Most everybody gets excited about cookies and other snacks. The fact is, people who snack together will work together. I would rather focus most of our energy on preparing for outreach than on preparing a meal.

Another method used to make outreach fun is the focus on testimonies. We want to know what blessings God has given to us as a result of outreach.

We continue to be amazed at how many God-ordained encounters occur. God seems to orchestrate the teams He wants to use for specific circumstances. One example of that would be an evening when a particular woman on one of our teams came to outreach a few days after her mother passed away. That evening when she arrived at the home of the unchurched person, she discovered that the prospect had lost her own mother two days earlier and was having a difficult time coping with the loss. God used the woman on our team, sharing with a broken heart, to touch the life of another woman who had strayed from Christ. Week after week God provides "coincidences" like this one. G•R•O•W outreach is not only inspiring; it's fun!

We probably do a poor overall job of conveying to the world that serving Jesus Christ is fun.

We do a poor job of conveying to the world that serving Christ is fun. When it comes to church growth and excitement, "faith is venturing out to do what God wants done, even if nobody believes is can be done. The test of faith is whether one really ventures his life and soul on things hoped for. Does the vision compel the pilgrimage?"[1]

Faith is fun! The objective of the G•R•O•W outreach program is to encourage people to carry out the vision of evangelism and church growth through their own personal, spiritual pilgrimage. If we are to see the vision of growth become a reality in our churches, then what is normal is not acceptable. It requires hard work; it requires faith; it requires the empowering work of the Holy Spirit; but it is fun!

When the Atlanta Braves won the World Series in 1996, I remember David Justice, outfielder, saying there was no feeling in the world like winning the World Series. I guess that is true. There is no feeling like winning *period*! The same is true with evangelism and church growth. Nothing is more exciting than leading someone into a personal relationship with Jesus Christ. Nothing is more "fun" than reaping the harvest of people who join your church as a result of outreach.

I am sure winning the World Series was quite an experience, but I would not trade places with David Justice of the Atlanta Braves on Tuesday evenings. Tuesday night outreach has become a time of true expectancy for the members of West Jackson Baptist Church. Expectations are faith in action–faith that results in vibrant, positive, and growing churches. As I shared in the principle of sowing and reaping, expectancy is the fuel for faith. Take my word for it, outreach that is based on the Master's plan is fun. Just ask Peter, James, and John!

---

[1] Donald A. McGavran, and Winfield C. Arn, *Ten Steps for Church Growth* (San Francisco, CA: Harper & Row, Publishers, 1977), 117.

Chapter 4

Making Quality Time Greater Than Quantity Time!

I remember a man telling me that when it comes to investments and dividends, it is better to have a small piece of the big pie than a big piece of the small pie. One of the success drivers of G•R•O•W outreach is the application of this principle. People in our churches are extremely busy–probably too busy! But the fact is, their time is in great demand.

I remember surveying people at Grace Baptist Church regarding a commitment to outreach. I asked two questions. First: "Would you commit one hour on Tuesday evening every week to organized church outreach?" A few responded with an enthusiastic yes. A few more said yes with guilt-ridden consciences. But most would not commit to a serious weekly commitment because of other time demands. Less than 10 percent of our weekly Sunday School average attendance made an unconditional commitment to weekly outreach.

The second question I asked was this: "Would you make a serious commitment to join an outreach team that meets once a month?" The response was staggering. At least 75 percent of the adults surveyed cheerfully said yes. At that moment I became sold on the

The entire ministerial staff is present every week for G•R•O•W.

principle of "quality time over quantity time." With that principle in hand, we were able to enroll 60 percent of our average Sunday School attendance in our G•R•O•W outreach program. The following chart illustrates the breakdown of the outreach teams.

> **G Team (meets on the first Tuesday of the month)**
> **R Team (meets on the second Tuesday of the month)**
> **O Team (meets on the third Tuesday of the month)**
> **W Team (meets on the fourth Tuesday of the month)**
>
> **When a fifth Tuesday occurs during a month,**
> **we invite the members of all teams to assist.**

When the same principle was applied to the outreach recruiting process at West Jackson Baptist Church, almost 50 percent of the average Sunday School attendance enrolled in the G•R•O•W program. Presently, we have more than three hundred enrolled in outreach.

One of the main keys to the success of the program is the priority placed on the Tuesday evening time of outreach. We allow no other meetings or activities to occur during that hour. No church-sponsored softball or basketball games are played during outreach. The entire ministerial staff is present every week for G•R•O•W.

I am sure the city thinks we're a little fanatical. When they schedule church league games, they simply do not schedule games from 7:00 to 8:00 on Tuesday evenings for teams at West Jackson Baptist Church. We want to convey to our church and community that the number one priority of West Jackson Baptist Church is evangelism and outreach. Setting aside an uncompromising time slot helps convey that priority.

**Desire alone
to see the church
grow is not enough.**

Only recently have churches begun to define their purpose and develop their own mission statements. McGavran and Arn pointed out, "The church of Jesus Christ is a big, broad Body and must not define its mission in terms of only one emphasis."[1] While we cannot limit our ministry as the church to only one mission endeavor, we must prioritize our mission statement. In order for an organized program of outreach to be effective, it must be at the top of the church's priorities. The principle of "quality time over quantity time" fosters enough grace that time demands do not have to limit a person's commitment to evangelism and outreach.

While the quantity of time spent by each member of the outreach program is lessened, strong accountability is placed on everyone regarding their one outreach night a month. That one outreach night per month is filled with hard but fulfilling work.

Peter Wagner based his book *Leading Your Church to Growth* on two principles. "First, the pastor must want the church to grow and be willing to pay the price. Second, the people must want the church to grow and be willing to pay the price."[2]

Desire alone to see the church grow is not enough. Church growth is hard work! The G•R•O•W outreach program will force the pastor and staff to reprioritize their time. The G•R•O•W program, more than any other avenue of ministry, educates our members to the way our staff spends their time. While I do not advocate abandoning in-reach ministries by the staff, a strong, organized, outreach ministry will force the congregation to adopt the philosophy of allowing the pastor and staff to make outreach a top priority.

Several months ago a deacon in the church brought up during a meeting that he wished the pastor and staff would attend more of the church-league basketball games. While the request was innocent

> **What is difficult is to prioritize your time in order to create growth.**

enough, it forced me to define my priorities of time management in a way I had not done before. Rather than become angry and defensive, I shared that the request would be honored. But I went on to explain that with the schedule already demanding 75–80 hours a week of my time, I would have to eliminate something. (At the time, I was visiting in the homes of at least four or five unchurched families per week.) I asked the deacons present to take official action requesting that some of the time devoted to personal evangelism and outreach be cut back in order to attend church-league basketball games. Needless to say, no one ever brought the issue up again. (And I was able to attend a few games that year.)

Most ministerial staffs would agree that it is not difficult to fill up a 40- to 50-hour workweek. What is difficult is to prioritize your time in order to create growth. The same is true with our congregations. When we ask for their time, we should do so with evangelism and church growth in mind. The "quality time is greater than quantity time" principle allows the average church member the flexibility to remain faithful to the evangelistic outreach ministry of the church and continue involvement in other ministry opportunities.

One last comment is in order regarding the teams that are created as a result of this principle. A healthy loyalty develops not only for the total outreach program but also for a person's team. The accountability is more defined. Rather than just letting the church down by their absence, they are letting their team down. That is why G•R•O•W is made up of teams that win! After all, we are simply carrying out the Master's game plan that is already a proved winner!

---

1 Donald A. McGavran and Winfield C. Arn, *Ten Steps for Church Growth* (San Francisco, CA: Harper & Row, Publishers, 1977), 67.
2 Peter Wagner, *Leading Your Church to Growth* (Ventura, CA: Regal Books, 1984), 44.

Chapter 5

Reaching Out by Divine Appointment

One Sunday evening in March 1994, just before we were to begin the evening service, Bob Brian, our minister of music at West Jackson Baptist Church, suffered a massive heart attack and passed away on the floor of the choir rehearsal room. Along with his dear wife and the youth choir with which Bob had been rehearsing, I looked on as paramedics attempted to revive him. Bob had been serving West Jackson Baptist Church for 14 years. Needless to say, I was not prepared to deal with my own grief, much less that of the church body. But God kept instilling in my mind one comforting thought. God assured me that, while this tragedy caught me completely off guard, it did not catch God off guard. Death, sickness, and pain certainly were not a part of God's original order of creation. But as a result of the fall, we encounter such tragedies as these. God's Spirit comforted me with the affirmation that He has orchestrated certain events of my entire life to prepare me to handle such events as losing my friend Bob Brian.

That same promise completely revolutionized my views of evangelism and outreach. The principle of "divine appointments" recognizes that God is already in the process of dealing with the hearts and lives of men, women, boys, and girls all over the world. The problem is that, unless we are in the "process of going," we may never encounter those divine appointments.

> **God is already in the process of dealing with the hearts and lives of men, women, boys, and girls all over the world.**

Nowhere in the Bible is this principle better illustrated than with Philip the evangelist in Acts 8:26-31: "And the angel of the Lord spake unto Philip, saying, Arise, and go toward the south unto the way that goeth down from Jerusalem unto Gaza, which is desert. And he arose and went: and, behold, a man of Ethiopia, an eunuch of great authority under Candace queen of the Ethiopians, who had the charge of all her treasure, and had come to Jerusalem for to worship, was returning, and sitting in his chariot read Esaias the prophet. Then the Spirit said unto Philip, Go near and join thyself to this chariot. And Philip ran thither to him, and heard him read the prophet Esaias, and said, Understandest thou what thou readest? And he said, How can I, except some man should guide me? And he desired Philip that he would come up and sit with him."

The story goes on to say that the Ethiopian surrendered to Christ and was baptized! What a story! God told Philip to "go" in verse 26 without telling him what was going to happen. What if Philip had not gone? What if he had demanded to see the plan before obeying? Well, for certain he would have missed the joy of leading the Ethiopian to faith in Christ.

A. T. Robertson said that the command of the Spirit for Philip to "join himself" in verse 29 had an interesting meaning. In the original language it means "to be glued to." He went on to say that the imperative use of the verb probably prompted Philip to jump on the running board on the side of the Ethiopian's chariot.[1] Wouldn't you love to have seen that? Philip was so eager to share his faith that he "ran" and jumped on the guy's chariot. Today Philip's actions might be perceived as too aggressive. But the fact is, a divine appointment was in process with the Ethiopian, and God needed Philip to testify of his own relationship with Jesus Christ. Philip didn't even need a

Not every visit, letter, call, or contact will be a divine appointment; but many of them will be!

marketing expert to locate the prospect. Because he was in the process of going, he experienced the principle of divine appointment.

Unless we mobilize and train our congregations to be in the process of "going," they will most likely overlook many God-ordained encounters of personal outreach and evangelism. Of course, an organized night of outreach is not essential to provide opportunities for witnessing; but experience suggests that those who are made aware of the need for intentional attempts to witness through an organized outreach program are also many times more likely to practice a continual lifestyle of evangelism. As a part of G•R•O•W, we like to see Tuesday evening outreach as a motivational tool that encourages people to witness every day.

Not all divine appointments are evangelistic in nature. God may place an outreach team in the home of a wife who is contemplating giving up on her marriage or a teenager considering suicide. The one needing a divine appointment may even be a cancer patient who was told on Tuesday morning that he has only a few months to live. Each of these examples has been reality on outreach nights at West Jackson Baptist Church.

Not every visit, letter, call, or contact will be a divine appointment; but many of them will be! The fact is, if we are not in the process of "going," we certainly will miss those appointments. I wonder how many divine appointments are missed daily because many churches do not have an avenue through which they motivate, mobilize, and train their members to recognize God's hand at work in the lives of people. Remember, divine appointments require us to be on time and in tune with the work of God's Spirit already in progress.

---

[1] Archibald Thomas Robertson, *Word Pictures in the New Testament*, vol. 3 (Nashville, TN: Broadman Press, 1930), 110.

Part II

Implementing the
G·R·O·W
Outreach
Program

Chapter 6

Casting and Catching the Vision

Grant Teaff, former head football coach at Baylor University, has always impressed me as a great motivator. He tells an interesting story of coaching at a smaller college in Texas. It seems that his team was to play a much stronger football team the following Saturday, and he was all tapped out of something to say that would motivate the team to play more intensely than ever before.

The team had acquired a stray dog that soon became the unofficial mascot for the team. His name was Ringer. Ringer slept from room to room, and the players had grown fond of the dog.

As Friday before the game rolled around, the appropriate words to motivate his team still had not surfaced. Before entering the double doors leading to the locker room where players were waiting, Coach Teaff noticed Ringer waiting by the door for the meeting to end.

Ringer had had a rather traumatic dating experience the night before when he had entered another dog's turf. His ear was cut; some of his hair was missing; and he had fresh blood around his eyes.

Just then the coach knew what he would say to the team. He managed to manipulate his face into an angry posture, picked Ringer up in his arms, and exploded through the double doors where the team was waiting. He sat Ringer down on a training table so all could see. With a quiver in his voice, his speech began, "Men, I don't know how

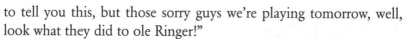

Motivation can be defined as "a force that propels into action."

to tell you this, but those sorry guys we're playing tomorrow, well, look what they did to ole Ringer!"

Needless to say, Coach Teaff's team played as never before and won the game. While this is probably not the kind of motivation most of us would do in our churches, it does point out an important fact. People can be motivated by words, actions, or events!

Motivation can be defined as "a force that propels into action." Everyone is not motivated by the same things, but everyone can be motivated. Our job as pastors is to motivate our people without manipulation. An effective, ongoing program of outreach and evangelism requires constant, heartfelt motivation from the pastor and staff.

I see Jesus as the Son of God, the King of kings, the Savior of the world, the Lord of lords; but I also picture Him as a "Master Motivator" when He walked this earth. Matthew 9:1-9 tells us about a sick man with palsy that Jesus healed. Jesus said two basic things to the sick man. First, verse 2 points out, Jesus said, "Son, be of good cheer; thy sins be forgiven thee." This bothered the religious gossips looking on because their feeling was that this man's sickness was a result of his sins. *After all,* they thought, *who was Jesus to release this man from the judgment of God?* But Jesus then said to the man, "Arise, take up thy bed, and go unto thine house." Sure, some looking on were angered by his audacity; others were impressed by his power; but a few were motivated by His love and compassion!

One of those few looking on was Matthew, the local IRS agent. Notice how Matthew responded to Jesus' miracles. "But when the multitudes saw it, they marvelled, and glorified God, which had given such power unto men. And as Jesus passed forth from thence, he saw a man, named Matthew, sitting at the receipt of custom: and he saith unto him, Follow me. And he arose, and followed him" (vv. 8-9).

I think the story goes down something like this. Jesus was back in His own city. As He walked through the streets, he saw the local IRS agent, or tax collector, working at his table. Jesus caught Matthew's eye as He walked by, but no words were exchanged. On up the way a block or so, Jesus healed this man with palsy. Everybody started carrying on and shouting, and Jesus was really not that comfortable with the shallow praise of those present. He simply turned and started walking back out of the city and once again caught the eye of one man, Matthew. Jesus stopped and with a loving but direct invitation said, "Follow me."

Matthew did! Even then Jesus knew this publican turned preacher would later give us perhaps the most detailed account of Jesus' life. Alfred Plummer said that Matthew's surrender was somewhat different from the other apostles. He was a tax collector under Herod Antipas; and while the position did not win him any public-relations awards, it was lucrative and easy to fill. Peter, James, and John could always return to their fishing, but not Matthew. "He risked everything by following Jesus."[1] Now that's motivation!

When I first acquired an interest in the game of golf, I accepted suggestions from anyone who knew anything about the game. I remember one particular golf pro trying to correct what had become a dangerous slice while driving the ball. For those who do not understand that term, a *slice* is when you hit a highly scientific, geometrical, but unintentional ball to the right, for a right-handed golfer. It was not dangerous for me but for the guys in the next fairway! When my golf-pro friend saw me, I had adopted the technique of a lot of new golfers. You know the routine. You line up and swing toward the left fairway, hoping that it lands in the center fairway of choice. He gave me an important piece of advice—after he stopped laughing, of

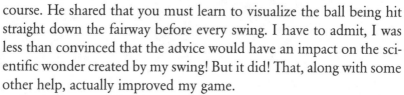

**Preaching should be
motivational as long
as it is biblically based.**

course. He shared that you must learn to visualize the ball being hit straight down the fairway before every swing. I have to admit, I was less than convinced that the advice would have an impact on the scientific wonder created by my swing! But it did! That, along with some other help, actually improved my game.

Proverbs 29:18 says: "Where there is no vision, the people perish." Vision is the outgrowth of expectancy discussed in chapter 1. Vision carries faith and expectation to the point of actually seeing the harvest before the harvest is given. Casting the vision goes a step beyond that. It motivates the congregation to see the harvest before the harvest is given!

A lot of us feel we cast vision adequately. But if our congregations do not catch what we cast, then our effort has been futile. Our world today is filled with inspiring self-help, new-age slanted, motivational speakers. I am not suggesting that pastors join the circuit of such speakers. But we must realize that intentional, motivational efforts are a part of our ministry. Let me suggest some ways you may want to consider casting vision in a way that your congregation will catch it.

Preaching

Contrary to what some people think, preaching should be motivational as long as it is biblically based. Before beginning a recruitment campaign at West Jackson Baptist Church, I preached a four-message series dealing with personal and churchwide evangelism. Following are the title, text, and synopsis of each message.

Expecting a Miracle (Matt. 13:54-58).—The message focused on the principle of expectancy and faith. It concluded that God will respond to our faith-filled preparations in evangelism and outreach.

Ye Shall Be Witnesses (Acts 1:6-11).—Obviously the message dealt with the Great Commission. But a real emphasis was placed on the fact that these were the last words of Jesus. The questions of when, where, and how to do personal evangelism were addressed.

If I Be Lifted Up! (John 12:32-36).—This message attempted to lay the foundation for the basic philosophy of our outreach ministry. It focused on keeping Jesus lifted up in every ministry of our church. We want our growth program not to market the church but to market Jesus!

When the Saved Stand Before the Savior (2 Cor. 5:10).—The message used the theme of 1 Corinthians 3:11-13 that deals with the kind of structure we build as believers on the foundation of Jesus Christ. It also listed the areas in which we will be evaluated and receive rewards from the Savior.

Sunday School Meetings

At the risk of sounding like a minister of education, let me say that the pastor must spend time instilling the vision of growth and evangelism in the minds and hearts of Sunday School leaders. I have found that casting vision is faster and more effective through leadership of the congregation than using the shotgun approach during the sermon. In many cases, Sunday School members have more confidence in their teachers than they do a new pastor. If the pastor can motivate those teachers and cultivate them to the point that they catch the vision of growth, then he has extended the growth agent beyond himself.

I have found that meeting with all the Sunday School leaders once a month on Sunday morning before the Bible study begins is a well-

> **Give the congregation enough time to catch the vision you are casting!**

attended time structure for the workers. The pastor can use the meeting time to cast his vision and to give well-deserved affirmation to the workers before the day begins. They leave the meeting appreciated, excited, and prepared to motivate their own classes to grow. I might also add that our teachers and workers assist in the goal-setting process during this time. They share successes and failures in an atmosphere of positive reinforcement. The weekly planning meetings become the time devoted to assist them with lesson planning and organization. The monthly meeting is strictly a time for the pastor and staff to prioritize and dream with Sunday School leaders.

One on One

As in the case discussed earlier with Matthew, Jesus did most of His personal discipleship and motivation in one-on-one relationships. Preaching and Sunday School meetings cannot take the place of sincere one-on-one fellowship with the leaders of the congregation. The vision may not be caught right away; but when congregational leaders get a bird's-eye view of your personal commitment to outreach and growth, they will be more likely to see your plan as more than passing fanfare. The pastor must initiate this one-on-one fellowship. That will convey to the target individual your sincere confidence in his or her ability and faith.

The time from starting to cast vision until the first official night of outreach will probably take from two to four months. Give the congregation enough time to catch the vision you are casting!

[1]Alfred Plummer, *An Exegetical Commentary on the Gospel According to St. Matthew* (Grand Rapids, MI: 1982), 138.

Chapter 7

Building a Fertile Prospect File

When my wife and I lived in Tullahoma, Tennessee, we enjoyed a nice home setting just outside the city. The only difficulty with the place was one little spot just outside our back door. It would not grow grass! There was no lack of effort. I tilled, sowed, fertilized, and watered but to no avail. The thing that finally helped was bringing in several inches of new, fertile top soil. The problem was not my lack of effort or the quality of the Kentucky 31 Fescue seed applied. It was the soil! It simply was not fertile.

An often-overlooked area that leads to the collapse of what seems to be a good plan of outreach is the quality of the prospect file. The prospect file must be fertile! A good prospect file allows us to concentrate our efforts in soil that will most likely produce some kind of harvest. This is not an advocation of a type of selective evangelism. It is simply an attempt to find the fields in which the Holy Spirit has already done preparation. This concept is derived from the fifth principle of "divine appointment" discussed in chapter 5.

A good example of the search for fertile fields is found in Acts 16:9-10: "And a vision appeared to Paul in the night; There stood a man of Macedonia, and prayed him, saying, Come over into Macedonia, and help us. And after he had seen the vision, immediately we endeavoured to go into Macedonia, assuredly gathering that the Lord

Developing a fertile and
active prospect file requires
the use of several avenues
through which you may
gather critical information.

had called us for to preach the gospel unto them."

This "Macedonian call" experienced by Paul, Dr. Luke, and the others on the journey was divine in nature. Luke, writer of Acts, was surely on this journey since he used the first-person, plural pronoun in verse 10.

Their obedience in going to Macedonia was met with some resistance. Luke recorded in verses 20-24 that they were beaten and thrown into jail. As the result of a midnight prayer meeting, God responded with an earthquake that freed Paul, Silas, and the other prisoners. But they all kept their place. Robertson said that the guard "left the other prisoners inside, feeling that he had to deal with these men whom he had evidently heard preach or had heard their message as servants of the Most High God as the slave girl had called them."[1]

The interesting note is that the field for their outreach and evangelism had become a jail. God had uniquely fashioned their travel plans in order for them to be at a jail in Philippi in order for the Philippian jailer to hear the message and commit his life to Christ. This is a critical point! The prospect file of your outreach program must be formed through much prayer and preparation in order for your outreach teams to be sowing, cultivating, and watering in fertile fields on outreach night.

Developing a fertile and active prospect file requires the use of several avenues through which you may gather critical information. I will share a few techniques through which we have built a healthy prospect file.

One of the most fruitful methods of assimilating prospects is through an in-house prospect search.

In-House Prospect Search

One of the most fruitful methods of assimilating prospects is through an in-house prospect search. It involves asking members of your congregation to do an evaluation of their friends, family, and neighbors who are unchurched. You will have to develop a relationship of trust in this area. If members become embarrassed by the way a prospect has been treated or approached by one of the outreach teams, that word will spread quickly; and your in-house search method will be dead!

During the messages used to cast vision, I suggest placing boxes or some other receptacles around the church to collect names of prospects from that point forward. For at least four Sundays in the organizing stage of the program, we place G•R•O•W Prospect Search cards in the orders of worship for Sunday. As the success of the program grows, you will find that your congregation will continue to turn in information on prospects. We always keep a supply of prospect search cards available to the congregation. (See illustration 1, Prospect Search Card, in the appendix.)

Special Events Registration

Except for funerals and weddings, if people come to our church for an event, we register their attendance. As is the case with many churches, we register the attendance of everyone present during worship services. Unless the entire congregation registers their attendance, persuading visitors to do so is difficult. The special form used for this registration is attached to our order of service and can easily be torn off and collected. Because West Jackson Baptist Church is in a strong growth pattern, about 65 percent of our prospects are first registered in a worship service. That compares with only 20 percent when the program first began. The guest registration card provides the opportunity for guests to request information about selected areas of our ministry. (See illustration 2, Sunday Worship Registration Card, in the appendix.)

Musicals.—Many churches provide at least one or two special musical events each year to which the community is invited. We have a special registration card used for all musical events at which attendance is registered by everyone, even members. (See illustration 3, Special Events Registration Card, in the appendix.) It also provides an avenue for those present to record spiritual decisions that may have been made as a result of the service. A good amount of planning and coordination has to be done in order to collect the information in an efficient manner during the service.

Children's outreach activities.—We occasionally plan special children's activities for the sole purpose of meeting unchurched children and families. One such example is Octoberfest sponsored by West Jackson Baptist Church every fall. While it serves as an alternative to the celebration of Halloween, its main purpose is definitely outreach. Game booths are provided by Sunday School classes. Candy and prizes are collected weeks in advance. There is absolutely no charge for the event. Children receive free candy and prizes. But in order to obtain tickets to participate in the games, they are required to complete a registration card that can be used for G•R•O•W outreach. The activity generates numerous contacts that require short-term and long-term cultivation.

Newcomers list.—A less-productive method of collecting prospects is using a newcomers list provided for a small charge by many orga-

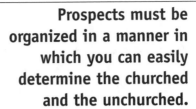

Prospects must be organized in a manner in which you can easily determine the churched and the unchurched.

nizations. While some churches do visit names collected from newcomers lists, we use the address simply to write a personal letter from the pastor and include brochures containing information about the ministries of our church. Immediate visits in these homes usually do more harm than good in cultivating prospects.

Once prospects are collected, they must be organized in a manner in which you can easily determine the churched and the unchurched. Non-Christian prospects should be assigned to someone capable of making a gospel presentation on outreach night. While all G•R•O•W members are trained to share their faith and the plan of salvation, others receive specialized training in personal evangelism. Such methods as the FAITH Sunday School Evangelism Strategy and CWT (Continuous Witness Training) offer wonderful approaches.

G•R•O•W visitation teams should have a prospect form that provides information that allows them to become well-acquainted with the prospect before the visit. The prospect form used by our G•R•O•W teams even includes information about previous contacts or visits. (See illustration 14, G•R•O•W Visitation Form, in the appendix.)

Most church growth pastors agree that an active, fertile prospect file is imperative to the success of any outreach program. You have heard it said that a chain is only as strong as its weakest link. The same is true with G•R•O•W outreach. A weak, unattended prospect file will certainly lead to the death of any outreach program.

---

[1]A. T. Robertson, *Word Pictures in the New Testament*, vol. 3: *The Acts of the Apostles* (Nashville, TN: Broadman Press, 1930), 262.

Chapter 8

Building Teams That Win

The philosophy behind building outreach teams is consistent with my overall philosophy of building leadership in other areas of ministry. Some people are followers, and others are leaders. Most people in our congregations fit into one of these two categories. As the shepherd of the congregation, the pastor is in the best position to determine who will be the best chiefs and who will be the best Indians. This chapter focuses on selecting captains and recruiting team members.

Selecting Team Captains

Certain people in the congregation can always rally the troops if necessary. This can, of course, be good or bad. If these people meet the qualifications that follow, they can help make the outreach program successful.

Typically the best captains for outreach are already serving in other capacities. Does that mean you should find someone else? Definitely not! First, the time demands on the group captains are not overwhelming. Second, if outreach is the priority we say it is and I must choose where I want my best leaders, it will be outreach! The best potential captains are usually already serving in some leadership

Captains cannot be volunteers; they must be hand selected.

capacity such as deacon, teacher, director, or officer. Growth-minded Sunday School teachers make excellent team captains, for they are already in a vision-casting position.

Each team should have at least two captains. After the enrollment reaches 40 for any given team, the team should add another captain for each additional 20 people. This limits the overall time that any one captain must spend recruiting or contacting team members.

Using this rule of thumb, the teams would always have one captain for every 20 people enrolled on their team. The only exception to this captain-participant ratio is that each team should start with at least two captains even if there are only 20 people on the team. This ensures that one captain can always be present if the other cannot.

Captains cannot be volunteers; they must be hand selected. When contacting a potential captain, allow enough time to share your vision and confidence in this program of outreach. Share your entire plan before asking the person prayerfully to consider becoming a captain. Captains do not rotate or have specified tenures. They serve as long as they are effective and willing. West Jackson Baptist Church now has 16 captains in its outreach program. The original eight are still serving after three years.

Understanding Qualifications for G•R•O•W Captains

Someone who is a leader of people outside the church is not necessarily qualified to be a G•R•O•W captain. Here are four essential qualifications for each captain.

Servant minded.—When I consider leadership ability and selection, I find it difficult to overlook what happened with Jesus and the disciples in the upper room in John 13. Verses 3-5 give us a beautiful picture of leadership and servanthood. "Jesus knowing that the Father had given all things into his hands, and that he was come from God, and went to God; he riseth from supper, and laid aside his garments; and took a towel, and girded himself. After that he poureth water into a basin, and began to wash the disciples' feet, and to wipe them with the towel with which he was girded."

Jesus was illustrating the kind of leadership philosophy on which He intended to build the church. Jesus washed the feet of those whom He knew would deny and betray Him. His leadership style was servanthood!

Captains for G•R•O•W must be capable of rolling up their sleeves and modeling servanthood leadership. They must be willing to help others carry out the Great Commission. Robert Coleman has stated in reference to the way Jesus selected His leaders, "His concern was not with programs to reach the multitudes, but with men whom the multitudes would follow."[1]

G•R•O•W outreach is not about a program but about people— people who, knowingly or unknowingly, have the capacity to turn the world upside down for Jesus Christ! While people may be impressed with our strength, they will be moved by our humility and servant- hood. It is imperative that G•R•O•W captains possess a servant's heart!

Encouraging.—One of my favorite people in the Bible is Barnabas. Acts 15:36-41 records a disagreement between Paul and Barnabas in relationship to whether John Mark could go on the next mission trip. John Mark had made some kind of mistake, and Paul had lost confi- dence in him, consequently not permitting him to participate in the upcoming mission trip. Barnabas, being an encourager, thought that John Mark could be of service. Whatever problem he may have had before, Barnabas felt this young man was still useful; and Barnabas was right! After all, John Mark has given us an early and reliable account of the life and ministry of Jesus in his Gospel and no doubt played an important role in the direction of the early church.

If you can find a Barnabas in your church, he will be an ideal G•R•O•W team captain. The atmosphere on G•R•O•W night must be exciting and filled with positive reinforcement. Participants should be present out of a sense of loyalty and commitment. While guilt-driven motivation is not always bad, it is not the best motivator for outreach. Team captains who are encouragers can motivate team members in an effective and positive manner.

Committed.—Captains should be so committed that they feel the same passion for outreach as the pastor and staff. Being from a coaching background, I like to call it "fourth quarter" commitment. It is the kind of commitment that, even though you may be down by 21 points in the fourth quarter of the game, you play as if heaven and hell are both shaken by your winning the game! Actually, that is the case with evangelism and outreach. You need captains who are committed even when the results are not immediate, captains who perceive obstacles as opportunities and who trust God with the simplest areas of their lives.

Love motivated.—There are two reasons that surely must motivate any of us to do the work of evangelism and outreach—love for the Savior and love for the sinner. One of the important characteristics of the G•R•O•W outreach program that must spread from top to bottom is love motivation. Too much of our church activity and service is task motivated rather than love motivated. Task motivation may be acceptable in some things we do, but it is not acceptable in the work of evangelism and outreach. A genuine love for Christ and the unchurched is essential to a successful growth program. Team captains must display commitment that is based on that kind of motivation.

The quality of the G•R•O•W team participant begins at the top of the organization. Captains for the teams should be the most visionary, servant-minded, encouraging, committed, love-motivated people in the church! They must be people capable of modeling the type of attitude and commitment you desire.

Training the Captains

Captains do not need to complete the entire four-week training separate from the participants. They simply should be training for what they will be asked to do. (See illustration 4, G•R•O•W Captains, in the appendix.)

Recruitment.—Captains should be given the specific expectations for their work. If four teams are used, each set of captains should be responsible for recruiting a number that is the equivalent of 10 percent of the average Sunday School attendance. For a church averaging 100 people weekly in Sunday School, an admirable response for each team would be 10 people. For a church with a weekly average attendance of 500, each team would do well to have 50 people. Captains should understand not only the numerical goals for each team but also the kind of loyalty and commitment desired from outreach team members.

Follow-up.—The follow-up aspect of the captains' responsibility comes in two ways. First, they are continually to recruit new members of the church or new Christians to participate in G•R•O•W outreach. Second, captains are responsible for contacting their teams on a monthly basis to remind them about outreach. The times and meth-

> **The recruiting process must be marked by a positive spirit that expects to succeed.**

ods used for ongoing recruitment could vary from church to church. Regardless of how you choose to do follow-up, your captains should be trained for the job. The responsibility of serving as a team captain may not require an enormous amount of time, but it does require a high level of faith and dedication!

Building the Teams

Most Christians agree that the greatest experience in life is the feeling of placing one's life at the foot of the cross and experiencing the saving knowledge of Jesus Christ. The second greatest feeling in the world is leading someone into that personal relationship with Christ. G•R•O•W provides the avenue through which Christians can play a role in the eternal lives of others. The pastor and staff should realize that this is not an ordinary recruitment campaign. The recruiting process must be marked by a positive spirit that expects to succeed. People will respond if they sense sincere commitment and excitement for the program. Four avenues should be used for the team-building process.

One-on-one recruitment.—One of the most effective team captains in the recruiting process for West Jackson Baptist Church still serves in our outreach ministry. He is the head baseball coach at one of our local colleges. He understands recruiting! When I shared with our captains that the most effective method for recruiting would be one-on-one conversations with members, Coach Cates responded, "I think I can handle that."

By the following Sunday he had met his goal for the recruitment process. He simply went to people and explained that he had an opportunity for them to commit to something exciting and thought

The entire church staff and other church leaders are expected to participate in the outreach program.

they might enjoy being a part of the team. While one-on-one conversation is not the only method for recruiting, it is the most effective.

Sunday School enlistment.—Since Sunday School plays such a vital role in the numerical and spiritual growth of the local church, it stands to reason that it should also be used in the G•R•O•W outreach ministry. Any small-group organization in the church could serve the same purpose in outreach. The ideal scenario is for each small group or Sunday School class to be represented each week during outreach. The minimum representation would be twice a month. The teacher or leader of the small group is the person in the best position to assist in this recruiting.

Leadership enlistment.—The entire church staff and other church leaders are expected to participate in the outreach program. Presently at West Jackson Baptist Church, a person is not allowed to serve as an active deacon in the church unless he is committed to our G•R•O•W outreach ministry. Since the outreach program is so diverse in its opportunities, there is a practical entry level for any member of the fellowship, especially key leaders.

Pulpit enlistment.—Pulpit enlistment is probably the most widely used method for recruiting in the average church. It is also the least effective! The pulpit serves best by informing, motivating, and preparing people to serve. A more personal form of enlistment usually nets a more stable and reliable commitment.

In most cases, at least with the general laity of the church, the enlistment campaign solicits a commitment to attend the four-week training before the actual commitment to the program is made. This gives participants a chance to view the program and expectations before making the final commitment to a team.

The practical success of the program rests on a quality, up-to-date prospect file.

Determining How Many Teams You Will Use

The practical success of the program rests on a quality, up-to-date prospect file; and I have discovered that many churches are located in communities where weekly outreach would oversaturate the prospect base. That being the case, it would be better to create two strong outreach nights a month rather than four weak ones.

Recently, I assisted a church in establishing a G•O program that applied all the same principles of G•R•O•W to an outreach program with two teams instead of four. The G•O program has had admirable results! The most successful element of the G•R•O•W outreach program has been its ability to be applied to practically any size church and community.

Remember, the most important elements in building teams that win are personal contact, love-motivated enthusiasm, expectation for success, and a willingness to make the program applicable to your fellowship of believers. You cannot train a team to win until you have recruited a team that desires to win and is willing to pay the price for victory!

[1]Robert E. Coleman, *The Master Plan of Evangelism* (Old Tappan, NJ: Fleming H. Revell, 1973), 21.

Part III

Training the Teams

Chapter 9

Session 1

Although the desire to witness for Jesus Christ should come naturally for every believer, certainly the ability to share a witness effectively doesn't always come that easily. Jesus spent the course of three years training twelve men to do effective outreach and evangelism. Three years for twelve men! Can you believe that? How much time has your church spent in "training" effective witnesses? I am convinced that many of us do an adequate job of motivating our churches to be more involved in personal evangelism, but we do a poor job of training people for the mission.

This chapter begins the actual training sessions for G•R•O•W outreach. We will present every detail of each of the four sessions. These training sessions have proved to be most successful when done on a Sunday evening prior to the worship service. This four-week training should take precedence over any other church programming during those four weeks. Participants should be seated around tables to enhance note taking, and the setup of the room should be conducive to dialogue. Each session requires at least 55 minutes. Allow ample time for questions during each session.

During the first training session many participants may be a bit timid about what they are being asked to do. Make sure the room is warm and inviting. In this first session the participants are asked to observe outreach and evangelism from the perspective of heaven and not earth. Many people see evangelism as something they *should* do

The focus and motivation of the training should be positive.

rather than as something they *get to* do. The focus and motivation of the training should be positive. The leader should be honest about his own frustrations in the areas of evangelism, outreach, and church growth.

The History of G•R•O•W

The most important thing that can be said about G•R•O•W at this point is that it works! I watched a church in complete disarray in Tullahoma, Tennessee, grow from an average Sunday School attendance of just over 60 people weekly to an average of more than 400 in two and one-half years. West Jackson Baptist Church in Jackson, Tennessee, has seen its average attendance for Sunday School climb from 470 to more than 840 in four years. With the consistent weekly contacts through G•R•O•W, the church enjoys the excitement of more than 100 visitors each week!

Churches all over the country are experiencing tremendous growth and excitement because this program will work in any community and any church which desires to grow and reach people. One pastor whose church has recently implemented the G•R•O•W program called to say he was overwhelmed by the response of his own people to the program. He said, "Our people see this program as something they can do!" His church in Texas enrolled more than 400 people in G•R•O•W within three months. The results of this program have proved that it is practical, flexible, and successful!

> **God will not bless where there has been no sowing or preparation.**

Principles of G•R•O•W

As part 1 of this book indicates, there are five guiding principles behind the G•R•O•W outreach program that produce success. I will give only a brief description of each principle here, since an entire chapter has already been devoted to each one.

Sowing and reaping.—The first principle is based simply on God's biblical principle of harvest. We cannot and should not expect a harvest where there has been no work. We should not expect a harvest when there has been no sowing. God will not bless where there has been no sowing or preparation. The expectation of harvest must be preceded by a season of labor. This is not the world's principle; it is God's principle!

Involving every member.—One of the greatest hindrances to most witnessing programs is that people do not feel adequate or comfortable sharing their faith with strangers. This fear translates into never committing to a program in which they would be trained to do such personal evangelism. G•R•O•W is built on the principle that every member of the congregation could be involved and not be asked to do something with which they would be uncomfortable. Once they are active participants in the G•R•O•W program, they begin to move toward different levels of involvement.

One of our most active members of G•R•O•W who regularly shares his faith said that he probably would never have committed to a "visitation only" outreach program. The entry level of writing letters gave him an avenue to participate without being pressured immediately to do something that was completely uncomfortable at the time. This particular man credits the "every member involvement" principle for providing an entry level of outreach that later took him to the

> **The principle that "outreach is fun" is predicated on the priority placed on outreach and evangelism.**

level of sharing his faith one-on-one in the home of a complete stranger.

Having fun with outreach.—This principle is where the change of mind-set comes in. This program is intended to move people from obligation participation to success-driven, enthusiastic participation. We communicate to our G•R•O•W team members that we expect them to have fun. If they don't, we do not ask them to come back.

Outside of the actual worship event on Sunday, outreach night is my number one priority. All other personal and church-related events are planned around outreach nights at West Jackson. The principle that "outreach is fun" is predicated on the priority placed on outreach and evangelism.

Anticipation and preparation for the adventure help make a vacation fun and exciting. Anticipation and preparation also make outreach fun!

Making quality time greater than quantity time.—Of all the five principles of G•R•O•W outreach, this one is the most popular among laypeople and the least popular among pastors. But the level and consistency of participation will be greater when you ask for only one hour a month rather than an hour each week. People who cannot commit to a night of outreach each week *can* commit to an hour of outreach each month. We ask for 15 hours a year!

Practically every member of the church could give 15 hours a year to outreach and evangelism. When we simply ask people to come every week if they can, the expectation is not clear. When the expectation is not clear, performance is sporadic. When participants become G•R•O•W team members, their expected performance is clear—one hour a month! If they cannot participate on their Tuesday one particular month, they are asked to make up the absence on another Tuesday evening. In this case it certainly has been proved that "quality time is greater than quantity time."

Reaching out by divine appointment.—I like to call this our "faith" principle. The principle of "divine appointment" assumes that God, through the Holy Spirit, is already at work in the hearts and lives of individuals. It suggests that coercion and manipulation are not legitimate tools for evangelism and outreach. If we are in the process of "going" as commanded by Jesus in Matthew 28:19, then we will encounter "hot spots" where the Holy Spirit is already at work. A "divine appointment" occurs when a willing witness, in the process of going, intersects with a tender, convicted heart. Every single aspect of the G•R•O•W ministry, from letter writing to phone calls and visits, is based on this faith principle.

Qualifications of G•R•O•W Team Members

While the G•R•O•W program is designed to involve practically every member of the fellowship, some people in the church, by their own choice, are not qualified participants. We emphasize three basic qualifications for every team member.

First, we ask that all members know for sure that they have truly had a "born again" experience with Jesus Christ, that they do not have any doubt about their eternal home in heaven and their relationship with Christ. Since we are in the "eternal life" insurance business, we insist that every participant has obtained the insurance we are promoting. Promoting such an experience would be difficult if you had never had the experience yourself!

Second, we ask each participant to commit to being present at G•R•O•W 12 times a year. Some church members will want to enroll

> **Love for the Savior and sinner should be the primary motivation for each G•R•O•W team participant.**

and simply show up when their schedule permits. Those who fit this category tend to do more to harm the momentum of outreach and evangelism than they do to propel it. For that reason, we ask that those who cannot honestly make the necessary commitment wait until circumstances allow them to fulfill this qualification. After all, few coaches, if any, would allow a player to participate on a team when they could not commit to any more than one or two games a year.

Third, participants need to be correctly motivated! Paul said, "Though I speak with the tongues of men and of angels, but have not love, I have become as sounding brass or a clanging cymbal" (1 Cor. 13:1, NKJV).[1] In the entire chapter Paul emphasized the prerequisite of "love" before ministry. This *agape* love Paul referenced was a term the early Christians adopted as an expression that described the intrinsic motivation of God and Christians to serve and give to others unselfishly. Obviously, G•R•O•W team members should be motivated by this kind of love. This love should be expressed first for the Savior, followed by love for the sinner, or those we are attempting to reach. Christians should love their church, pastor, and staff. All members should desire to see their church grow. But love for the Savior and sinner should be the primary motivation for each G•R•O•W team participant. (See illustration 5, G•R•O•W Enrollment Card, in the appendix.)

Avenues of Outreach Through G•R•O•W

During the first session, overview what team members will be asked to do. More details about these responsibilities will be given in later sessions. The following avenues for outreach are just an overview of

> **A visitation program that does not seek to share the gospel is nothing more than a church marketing campaign.**

what happens on G•R•O•W night.

Visitation.—Intentional, organized, effective visitation is not an outdated method of outreach and evangelism. Even though all participants will not choose to be involved in this aspect of G•R•O•W outreach, all participants will be trained in the following sessions to make at least three types of visits.

First, some participants will be assigned to make personal, evangelistic visits with the intention of making a gospel presentation. Not every visitor will be comfortable making this type of visit, but many will. Stress at this point that those making evangelistic visits will receive the necessary training for the task. A visitation program that does not seek to share the gospel is nothing more than a church marketing campaign. This segment of outreach is the "anchor" leg of the G•R•O•W outreach ministry.

Second, some participants will make church prospect visits. These visitors will be equipped with materials and training to educate and pray with prospects about their decision to become part of the church. Outreach and information materials will be developed and made ready for those making this type of visit.

Third, some participants will be asked to conduct crisis or care-giving visits. In a society experiencing an alarming rate of divorce, violence, and other tragedies, the church must respond to these needs. While the pastor, staff, and deacons frequently make these type visits, G•R•O•W outreach provides an avenue for the general laity to be involved as well. Many in our congregations are extremely gifted and capable of providing this type of ministry through G•R•O•W outreach.

Letter writing.—While sample letters and specific instructions are provided to each person involved in the letter-writing ministry, the

We have discovered that letters average two contacts per letter.

letters should be handwritten and personal. Most information and training about letter writing will be shared in a later session. Sample letters to possible newcomers, Sunday School absentees, first-time visitors, frequent visitors, special event visitors, bereaved, and even new births in the community are included in the G•R•O•W program. We have discovered that letters average two contacts per letter. As you can see, letter writing, when organized correctly, can be an effective way to make a large number of contacts each week. As a matter of fact, it is probably the most efficient use of time during the outreach night. (See illustrations 6-12, sample letters, in the appendix.)

Phone calls.—While the ability to use the phone on outreach nights requires some logistical planning, it can be effective if callers are adequately trained. Many prospects and visitors respond better to a phone call than a visit. For example, if a prospect visits your church two weeks in a row and receives an informative visit after the first week, a phone call after the second visit may be more appropriate than a home visit two weeks in a row. Absentee members usually respond to phone calls as well.

A Typical G•R•O•W Night of Outreach

A typical night of G•R•O•W outreach can be broken down into four segments.

First is the arrival and sign-in segment. All participants are asked to record their attendance and to indicate the area of outreach they will work in that evening. Those who already have a visitation partner will also note that on the sign-in sheet. (See illustration 13, G•R•O•W Sign-in/Roster, in the appendix.)

Second is the process of making assignments and welcoming the

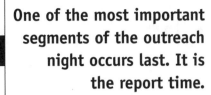

One of the most important segments of the outreach night occurs last. It is the report time.

participants. Most of the assignments should be made as people arrive so that once the welcome is made and prayer is offered by the pastor, team members can go to work. The welcome, assignments, and prayer can all be accomplished within five to seven minutes for up to one hundred participants. The church staff and G•R•O•W team captains assist in this segment of the outreach night.

Third is the actual work involved in the outreach night. The work segment of the night should be planned to use about 50 minutes.

One of the most important segments of the outreach night occurs last. It is the report time. This is the celebration part of G•R•O•W. Even those who have not had a successful visit or call can hear about others' success. For this time to be effective, reports should be limited to about 30 seconds. If not, the report time can become long, and participants will lose interest. The entire report time should not take more than 15 minutes. If the outreach night begins at 7:00, the team members should be on their way home by 8:15. Meeting this objective will require much planning and discipline, but team members will appreciate a consistent schedule!

---

[1] From the *New King James Version*. Copyright © 1979, 1980, 1982, Thomas Nelson, Inc., Publishers.

Chapter 10

Session 2

Your Most Valuable Tool for G•R•O•W Outreach

Session 2 should begin with the introduction of the most valuable tool for G•R•O•W outreach. That tool is the testimony of each participant. Paul's salvation experience is recorded in Acts 9:1-19 as well as in other places. Paul saw his own personal testimony of his encounter with Christ as his most important witnessing tool. Many Christians do not know how effectively to share with others their own personal salvation encounter with Jesus Christ. G•R•O•W training will equip participants to do just that!

The personal testimony of each Christian serves at least three specific purposes.

First, it proves the reality of grace. We are seeking to convince others that change is possible! that Christ is real! that heaven is attainable! Why? Because we have personally met the Savior of the world. A personal testimony proves the reality of God's grace.

Second, the personal testimony plants seeds in others' hearts and minds. For some reason, people remember others' actual experiences better than they retain mere facts. A personal testimony serves as a seed planted in the life of someone who hears it!

Third, dealing with personal testimonies during G•R•O•W training serves as a test of salvation for participants. If a participant has no personal testimony, then there is no experience of grace. If there is no experience of grace, then there is no salvation. This area of the G•R•O•W training has proved to be the most exciting.

G•R•O•W team participants should be asked to write their personal testimony for session 2. They should be asked to do so on one side of a sheet of paper. The testimony should be something they can share verbally in three to five minutes. While that may sound impossible to some, an initial testimony shared in that length of time will do more to elicit questions from an unbeliever than someone's entire life story. Also our daily lives seldom provide an opportunity of large segments of time to share with others.

Ask participants to share their personal testimony with someone else involved in G•R•O•W training. This allows them to practice organizing their thoughts as they verbally present what they have written. Remind team members that they are to share this information in three to five minutes. Participants should then be asked to share their personal testimony with at least one other person the following week.

When You Arrive at Outreach

If outreach begins at 7:00 p.m., participants are asked to arrive in plenty of time to sign in and be ready to begin at that time. As they arrive, team members should be greeted by group captains at a sign-in table. At this point they will post their attendance and mark their desired area of work for the evening (visits, letters, phone calls). They will be assisted by a group captain in being paired up for visitation if that is their role for the evening. They should receive a name tag and enter the G•R•O•W room. (A durable name tag should be provided for each participant.) Team members who are writing letters should be seated at the letter-writing tables. Participants making phone calls should go to the area designated for those assignments. Members making visits will report to the visitation assignment table.

> **Before leaving the parking lot, visitors should pray specifically for the family and the visit.**

The Visitation Assignment

As mentioned in session 1, those making visits may participate in soul-winning, prospect, or caregiving visits. For each type of visit, participants should sign in with a partner and receive a visitation assignment at the visitation table. They should familiarize themselves completely with the assignment. Information on the form will include names, address, ages, and comments about the family as well as reports involving previous visits. (See illustration 14, G•R•O•W Visitation Assignment Sheet, in the appendix.) A thorough review of the recorded information is time well spent for the visitation team. Familiarity with the information could prevent embarrassment. Maps showing the specific location should be attached to the assignment.

Each visitation assignment should have a "section" number assigned to it. The section number denotes the specific location in the city. A city or county map can be divided into 6, 9, or 12 sections. Plenty of copies of each section should be made and stored for each visit. While large maps should be posted in various places in the G•R•O•W room, making available small section maps will save a great deal of time to those attempting the visit. The section number of the prospect can be logged into the computer when the prospect is listed, or this process can be done by hand before outreach night begins.

Next, visitors should pick up appropriate materials to share information about the church and its ministries. Specific instructions about actually making the visit will be covered in session 3. Before leaving the parking lot, visitors should pray specifically for the family and the visit. Visitors should return to the church by 8:05 p.m. and sign in for the visitation report order. This will allow the staff and captains to know quickly who has and has not yet returned.

Visitors should carefully record information about the visit on the assignment sheet. This is critical! Since different teams will be going out each week, this information will be logged in and processed for future contacts.

Reporting on each visit should be limited to 30 seconds. At the conclusion of the report time, the assignment sheet should be turned in to the visitation assignment table.

Letter-Writing Assignments

Tables used for letter writing should be equipped with pens, stationary, envelopes, and any materials that may be included with the letter. Team captains should begin the distribution of the assignments by 6:50 p.m., assuming that outreach begins at 7:00 p.m.

Guests.—First-priority letters are usually to those who have visited the previous Sunday. Visitor registration forms will contain the names of the guests and are generally broken down into three categories: prospects, members of other churches, and out-of-town guests. Sample letters relate to each of these guests.

New residents.—Letters to new residents in the city are usually the next priority of letters written. A list of these newcomers can be obtained through various services such as utility companies, the chamber of commerce, or other groups who specialize in providing this type of list. Even if a cost is involved, obtain the most reliable list available.

Possible new residents.—Another type of letter to be written would be to a list of possible newcomers to the city. This list may be provided by the local chamber of commerce. Many possible newcomers will write the chamber of commerce for information about the city. They usually respond well to receiving an informative personal letter about your church and any other materials that might educate them about the ministries of your church.

Sympathy.—Another valuable ministry involves writing letters to those who have recently lost loved ones. It is best to time these letters to arrive between two to four weeks after the loss. A possible list for these letters may be obtained from local funeral homes. If funeral homes are reluctant to provide such a list, you can search the obituaries of local papers and use a city directory to obtain addresses.

Remember that the objective of these letters is to convey sympathy. This is not a prospect letter! I have discovered that most who experience loss due to death experience a lull in contacts from friends and family around two to four weeks after the loss. As you can see from the sample letter, the intention of this ministry is to assure those grieving of the church's love and prayers. If persons experiencing grief do not have a church home, they will be more likely to contact your church for support, having already received a letter.

Sunday School absentees.—G•R•O•W outreach is a tremendous avenue through which some of the Sunday School outreach can occur. If you succeed in having each class represented by someone each week, then absentee and other contacts can be made through cards and letters. Remember, even "in house" contacts will result in a higher average attendance among those who are already members.

As mentioned earlier, samples for each type of letter should be provided for those involved in the writing ministry. Included with the sample letters are guidelines for the writer to use in order for this ministry to succeed.

Callers should be sensitive to whether the timing of the call is convenient for the prospect.

Phone-Call Assignments

Specific areas for making phone calls must be established before the G•R•O•W outreach ministry begins. View the phone-call contact with the same objective as for those making personal visits. Phone-call assignments should be arranged and distributed by team captains at the assignment table. Callers should familiarize themselves completely with the information provided about prospects. The caller should be well acquainted with the various ministries of the church and be prepared to answer questions related to those ministries.

Callers should not be intrusive. They should be sensitive to whether the timing of the call is convenient for the prospect. Callers should be reminded to stick to the business at hand. It may help the caller to list an agenda for the call before it is made.

Results from the call should be recorded immediately after each call on the phone-call assignment sheet. These sheets should then be returned to the assignment table at the conclusion of outreach. Praiseworthy contacts should be reported during the report time.

Remember to allow ample time throughout session 2 for questions related to the assignments. Encourage participants to review the information about each area before the next session.

Chapter 11

Session 3

For the outreach program to succeed and maintain its integrity in the church and community, visitors in the G•R•O•W program must be trained to be sensitive to the people they are attempting to reach. Session 3 should be devoted entirely to the circumstances surrounding the visit. This preparation will not only equip visitation teams but will also build confidence in their ability to accomplish the mission. This session focuses primarily on soul-winning and prospect visits. Since caregiving visits vary from need to need, any instruction for these types of visits should be given outside the G•R•O•W training.

Preparing to Visit

Preparing to make the visit focuses on three areas: learning principles for visiting, establishing protocol for visiting, and making the visit.

Learning Principles for Visiting

Consider these five steps.

1. Set the time to go.—Obviously, the G•R•O•W program employs this principle by allowing an organized night of outreach. The mission of visitation, if not planned, usually never happens.

2. Don't be pushy.—Leave the door open for future visit. Ask the person if he or she would allow you to come inside for a brief time of discussion about your church. Allow the prospect to make that decision. Too much aggression may intimidate or irritate the prospect.

**Jesus Christ
has already earned
the right for His
story to be told!**

3. Don't embarrass the prospect.—I heard about a minister who recognized a non-Christian in a restaurant. Not wanting to miss the opportunity to witness, the minister interrupted the prospect's business lunch with questions that embarrassed the man. Needless to say, the encounter was not a "divine appointment." As a rule, if the prospect is embarrassed by your conversation, you have not handled the encounter appropriately.

4. Understand your authority base.—The visitation team does not go out under the authority of their church. G•R•O•W participants speak under the authority of Jesus Christ and His death on the cross. Jesus Christ has already earned the right for His story to be told!

5. Understand the principle of harvest.—You cannot expect harvest to occur unless sowing and cultivation have already taken place. One visit may sow; a letter may cultivate; and the harvest may not occur for weeks or months. The success of the visit should not be measured by immediate harvest.

At the completion of these principles, introduce skits that portray good and bad techniques of G•R•O•W visitation. One skit should focus on bad techniques by allowing someone to portray being too pushy. Another skit should portray how graciously to accept the fact that the timing is not right for the visit by agreeing to come back another time. A third skit could focus on a team successfully entering a home and using good methods for visitation.

Establishing Protocol for Visiting
Simple reminders can enhance your visit.

1. Be clean and neat.—Visitors should dress casually. Being overdressed could make the prospect uncomfortable, but being underdressed might result in the church's being embarrassed. Dress should

> **Participants, like the first disciples, need the fellowship of another laborer.**

communicate that the visit is informal but important.

2. Go "two by two."—In Luke 10:1, Jesus sent the disciples out two by two. While more visits could be made with the participants going out individually, this practice should be avoided. Participants, like the first disciples, need the fellowship of another laborer. Also, certain circumstances of the visit are easier when there are two. If children are in the home, one of the team members may be needed to occupy the children while the other directs conversation to the adults.

3. Be courteous.—If the prospect has company or is in the middle of an evening meal, the visitation team should graciously agree to come at another time. Your courteous response to an inappropriate time for the visit will reflect well on you, your church, and your Lord!

4. Don't be surprised by non-Christian behavior.—If prospects are not expecting your visit, they may not be prepared for you. Don't get bug-eyed by something in the home that you personally find offensive. Remember, a change of heart will result in a change of behavior. Don't expect the change of behavior to occur first.

5. Avoid verbal overkill.—Don't use language the prospect will not understand. Use terminology that communicates easily the nature of your visit. Using a word like *sanctification* may leave the prospect thinking you are referring to some type of medical procedure.

6. Be complimentary.—Find something about the person, home, or children that you can compliment honestly. This will help keep the visit from becoming confrontational.

Making the Visit
Think about these ideas before the visit.

1. Know names and family information.—The visitation assignment form should be detailed enough for the team to be familiar with

> **You cannot convey genuine interest in the prospect without listening to the prospect.**

prospects. This allows the visit to be more informal.

2. Decide who will lead.—Just as in dancing, someone must lead! A designated leader of the team for conversation will allow the time of the visit to be used more efficiently.

3. Go to the front door.—Contrary to popular opinion, back-door guests are not always the best kind! Don't assume the prospect will expect guests at the back door. Sticking by this rule will seldom place the visitor in an embarrassing situation.

4. Pray for the person you are visiting.—Before leaving the parking lot of the church, pause and pray for the visitation encounter. If our authority base is Jesus Christ, then we want to confess our dependence on Him for the success of the visit.

5. Prepare introductory remarks.—Without sounding as if the introduction is canned, state your name, your partner's name, and the church you represent. Ask for permission to enter the home for a brief visit. Returning for a second visit is better than attempting to cover additional information at the door.

6. Show genuine interest in the prospect.—You cannot convey genuine interest without listening to the prospect. Ask prospects questions they would enjoy answering. Family and jobs are generally good topics. And all grandparents enjoy talking about their grandchildren!

7. Have a conversation plan.—Our G•R•O•W participants are trained to use the acrostic FORM as a conversation plan.

F stands for questions you may ask about *family*.

O represents conversation about *occupation* or work.

R is for the the prospect's involvement in *religion* or church.

M stands for your *message* or the reason for your visit.

When visitors begin to discuss religion, they should ask prospects if they are members of any church. If they say yes, visitors should ask

Offer whatever help is needed to assist prospects in finding your church.

about their relationship with that church and the status of their present relationship with Jesus Christ. If prospects respond with no to the question of church membership, the visitor should then ask the prospects if they are Christians. Answers to these questions dictate your message or purpose for the visit. At this point visitors should be prepared to move down the path to one of two kinds of visits.

Two Kinds of Visits

Church-Centered Visit

If prospects seem confident about their saving relationship with Jesus Christ, then the visitor should begin to share relevant information about the church. Material containing information about the church should be used and left with the prospect. Here are some important guiding principles for this type of visit.

1. Love your church.—The prospect will be impressed by your genuine love and excitement about your church. Needless to say, visitors who do not love their local church or are not excited about its ministry should not be involved in this type of visit.

2. Ask for specific commitment.—Ask the prospect, "Can you visit with us this Sunday?" Visitors should offer to meet prospects at a designated location to make them more comfortable during their first visit to your church. Offer whatever help is needed to assist prospects in finding your church. Failure to ask for a specific commitment from the prospect lessens the success and impact of the visit.

3. Keep the visit brief.—The church-centered visit should not exceed 15-20 minutes. This is why the conversation plan is important. Except in unusual circumstances in which prospects express a need for additional help, they will appreciate your consideration of their time.

Don't push prospects to Christ; lead them to Christ!

Christ-Centered Visit

The Christ-centered visit requires more time. Information in session 4 will train participants to share the plan of salvation. Here are some brief guidelines to initiate this conversation.

1. Be sensitive to the Holy Spirit.—While prospects may not be Christians, they also may not be prepared to make a commitment to Christ on your visit. Plant seeds the Holy Spirit can use later, even if the prospect is not prepared to make a commitment to Christ during your visit.

2. Do not try to enter an "unopened door."—Don't push prospects to Christ; lead them to Christ! If prospects are not willing to commit their life to Christ, the best thing you can do is to leave a positive impression regarding your own relationship with Jesus Christ.

3. Ask for permission to share your personal testimony.—Developing in advance a presentation of your personal testimony will help you share your faith quickly and clearly. Initially the prospect will be more impressed by a personal account of someone who has met Christ than anything else you might share. This will open the door for questions from prospects and further discussion about their need for Christ. The next session will equip the participant with a gospel presentation that can be used from this point.

4. Report details of the visit.—If the prospect does not make a decision for Christ, you may not be the next person to visit in that home. Your detailed record with information about the conversation and your visit will help the next visiting team. An adequate report of your visit could determine the effectiveness of the next visit made with this prospect.

Chapter 12

Session 4

A standard scale accepted by most church-growth proponents for the diversity in evangelistic strategy has four levels—E-0, E-1, E-2, and E-3—of evangelization. Here is simple explanation of each level.

E-0.—A strategy or plan that is successful in reaching those who are already in the church. It basically revolves around biological growth or reaching our own children.

E-1.—A strategy or plan that is successful in reaching the neighborhood—people of the same homogeneous unit.

E-2.—A strategy or plan that succeeds in reaching people across a relatively small ethnic or cultural barrier. Crossing some racial and cultural barriers within one's own community would be an example of this level of evangelism.

E-3.—A strategy that is successful in reaching people across cultural, racial, and language barriers. While this level of evangelism may occur in one's city, it is most likely to occur in foreign mission efforts.

The G•R•O•W outreach program has proved effective when the goal of evangelization ranges from the E-0 to E-2 levels. Session 4 focuses on training participants to be active in personal evangelism whether through the G•R•O•W program or throughout daily activity.

Understanding the Basis for Going Out

G•R•O•W participants should realize that New Testament evangelism is ambitious and intentional rather than passive. Church-growth pro-

Most Christians admit that the thought of approaching a complete stranger and sharing a witness for Christ brings some anxiety.

ponents of lifestyle evangelism have never intended that Christians approach witnessing with a passive or nondirective style. Directives, or examples in direct styles of evangelism, can be found in Matthew 28:18-19, Acts 1:8, Acts 8:26-38, and Acts 16:9. Each of these references carries a direct, divine mandate to evangelize. We can certainly accept the conclusion that the divine mandate to reach our communities is no less direct or important.

Sharing a Witness for Christ

Fear of Witnessing

Most Christians admit that the thought of approaching a complete stranger and sharing a witness for Christ brings some anxiety. But fear in witnessing that completely prohibits Christians from sharing their faith may be linked to three basic causes.

1. Lack of personal assurance.–If Christians are not confident about their own personal relationship with Christ, they certainly cannot be comfortable sharing about that relationship with someone else. (The pastor may find it constructive to address the issue of assurance in messages being preached during the weeks of the G•R•O•W training.)

2. Personal sin.–If Christians are not in fellowship with Jesus Christ because of personal sin, they also may experience fear and apprehension in personal witnessing efforts.

3. Personal ego.–Believers must understand that their authority base for witnessing is not their own ability or power. A fear about what prospects may think of them after the witnessing encounter can create fear in witnessing.

> **Conversation that allows prospects to interact and to ask questions is the best method of personal evangelism.**

Methods of Witnessing

Throughout the New Testament two types of witnessing styles are employed for the purpose of evangelization.

1. Monologue.—The word frequently used in the New Testament for this style of witnessing is *karusso*. It denotes what is commonly accepted today as preaching. While this method of evangelism was used when addressing the masses, it was seldom employed as an effective style of one-on-one witnessing.

2. Dialogue.—The word used in the New Testament for this style of witnessing is *laleo*. The word refers to conversation between two or more people. Conversation that allows prospects to interact and to ask questions is the best method of personal evangelism.

Employing the Principle of Neutral Words

A neutral word that might be commonly used in daily conversation may lead into conversation or questions about spiritual topics. Examples of neutral words include *death, sickness, weather,* and *family*.

If a non-Christian mentions a situation involving the death of a friend or family member, the witness might say, "I'm not sure I personally could cope with that type of tragedy without trusting the Lord." A neutral word simply serves as a bridge to move the conversation from secular to spiritual. Most successful witnesses notice and take advantage of witnessing opportunities using neutral words.

Presenting the Gospel in a Nutshell

The following outline presentation is one that may be used to share the gospel. It focuses on four steps participants can easily remember.

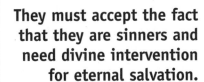

They must accept the fact that they are sinners and need divine intervention for eternal salvation.

Salvation needed.—The basis for "salvation needed" is Romans 3:23: "For all have sinned, and come short of the glory of God." For prospects to understand the meaning of *grace*, they must realize their need for grace. They must accept the fact that they are sinners and need divine intervention for eternal salvation.

Once this concept is shared and explained, the witness should use a transitional question to move to the next step. An example of such a transitional question for the prospect might be, Have there been times in your life when you have done things you know were disappointing to God?

If the prospect answers affirmatively, the witness should point out the result of sin mentioned in Romans 6:23, "For the wages of sin is death." The visitor should explain that "*wages*" refers to "penalty or consequences."

A question to be asked before moving forward is, Would you like me to share with you how God responds to our need for His help in this matter?

The witness should not move to the next step unless confident the prospect understands the need for salvation.

Salvation provided.—Romans 5:8 states, "God commendeth his love toward us, in that, while we were yet sinners, Christ died for us." God has provided an answer to our dilemma with sin. God loves us in spite of our sin and desires to have a relationship with us. Jesus Christ's death on the cross serves as the "payment" for our sins. The shedding of Christ's blood on the cross and our acceptance of that act of love can erase our error or sin.

Another question for the prospect should be used at this point: Would you be willing to allow Jesus Christ to do something for you that you cannot do for yourself?

> **By now the prospect should recognize that Jesus Christ was not merely a good man.**

By now the prospect should recognize that Jesus Christ was not merely a good man. He was the Son of God. God gave His own Son in order to adopt us as children through the process of salvation.

Salvation offered.—The last part of Romans 6:23 states, "But the gift of God is eternal life through Jesus Christ our Lord." The prospect should understand that the death of Christ on the cross was intentional and for the purpose of redeeming all people. It was not an abstract event in history that people have adopted as a saving event. It was by God's initiative and God's plan!

The witness might now ask the prospect, "Since the gift of eternal life is a gift and something we cannot earn or do for ourselves, would you be willing to receive this gift?"

If the prospect answers yes to this question, the witness should proceed with this question: Would you like for me to share with you how you can receive this gift?

Assuming the prospect answers affirmatively, the witness is ready to move to the next step.

Salvation accepted.—The witness should explain that in order to experience true forgiveness of sin, there must be true repentance or turning away from sin. If the prospect understands the meaning and importance of repentance, the witness may share Romans 10:9-10: "That if thou shalt confess with thy mouth the Lord Jesus, and shalt believe in thine heart that God hath raised him from the dead, thou shalt be saved. For with the heart man believeth unto righteousness, and with the mouth confession is made unto salvation."

The witness should make sure the prospect understands the meaning of these verses. Once that has happened, the witness may now ask the question, "Would you like for me to lead you in a prayer to confess your sin and accept Jesus Christ as your Savior?"

The new Christian should also be enrolled in a new Christian's discipleship class as soon as possible.

If the prospect is willing, the witness should lead the prospect in a simple prayer that covers all four steps of the gospel presentation. An example of such a prayer might be as follows: *Lord Jesus, I know that I am a sinner. I know that I have done things that have been wrong in God's eyes. I realize that Jesus died on the cross and rose again in order to save me. I accept that act of love on my behalf. I receive the gift of eternal life. Come into my heart, forgive my sin, and control my life. Thank you for saving me today!*

Once the prospect has completed this prayer, the witness will want to spend some time explaining the importance of prayer, Bible study, and spending time with other Christians in the fellowship of a local church. The witness will also want to ask for permission to share the prospect's decision with a minister for discussion about baptism and church membership. The new Christian should also be enrolled in a new Christian's discipleship class as soon as possible.

Only the Beginning

Completion of the G•R•O•W outreach training is not the end but rather the beginning of a wonderful new direction for the participants and their church. A genuine desire to reach the local community for Christ will also lead to a more intense desire to reach people through missions all over the world!

Part IV

Ensuring Success

Chapter 13

Preparing for the First G•R•O•W Night

Thom Rainer, in *Effective Evangelistic Churches*, said that "methodologies are important when we see them as tools to be used by God, rather than *the* perfect solution to our churches' needs."[1] If the reader senses that the G•R•O•W outreach program will be just the idea that "saves" his church from apathy and decline, he will meet disappointment. Methodologies like G•R•O•W are not "fix it" solutions to deep problems of division, decline, and disillusionment in the congregation.

Unfortunately, many couples feel that children are the answer to difficulties in their relationship. As they soon find out, the addition of children as a "fix it" sometimes even compounds the problems. But to a healthy marriage relationship, children can make the home stronger and certainly exciting. And so it goes with G•R•O•W. Even though the church may be stagnant and complacent, if it is healthy and focused, the G•R•O•W outreach problem can serve as God's tool to point the fellowship in the right direction and allow the church to experience success in carrying out the Great Commission.

After reviewing the content of the training sessions contained in part 3, we point our attention to some items of detail that, along with the implementation schedule, will assist the reader in preparing for the first night of G•R•O•W.

> **The prospect file is the fuel for the fire.**

Setting the Target Date

The "target date" is the date you want to schedule your first night of G•R•O•W outreach. The pastor and staff will need to allow 12-14 weeks for the implementation of G•R•O•W. This timetable includes the four-week training. (See 14-Week Calendar in the appendix.)

Fall or spring is a good time to begin G•R•O•W. Assuming the leader sets a night in October as the target date, then the implementation schedule should begin in July. If the target date is in March, the implementation schedule should begin in December.

I have found it helpful to set the target date at the same time as a special high-attendance day or revival. This move generates several excellent prospects that serve as tremendous fuel for the first few weeks of the program. Everything in the planning and promotion of the process should point toward the target date.

Planning a Successful Report Time

These tips will keep your report time brief and exciting.

• Limit the total time devoted to reporting on visits to a maximum of 15 minutes.

• Have visitation teams sign in when they return to the church. This lists provides the reporting order. This encourages different people to report each week.

• End at the same time each week. Failure to follow through with this commitment will lead some participants to leave early.

• Celebrate! That's the purpose of the report time!

If you want young couples involved in the G•R•O•W outreach program, you will need to provide child care.

Maintaining the Prospect File

The prospect file is the fuel for the fire. Work on the prospect file for visitation should begin immediately! Necessary steps toward obtaining a newcomers list and other components of the prospect file should not be delayed. The in-house prospect search covered earlier should be promoted and run throughout the implementation process. While a prospect file kept manually and updated by hand can be used, a computer program that allows you to print potential visits and update records quickly will be well worth the investment.

Recruiting Team Captains

A great amount of prayer and consideration should be given to recruiting team captains. They should know and feel that the initial success of G•R•O•W rests on their shoulders. Their excitement and commitment to the program will determine their level of success in recruiting participants.

The pastor and staff should spend as much time as necessary to train and educate these captains about the program and implementation schedule. This delegation of leadership and responsibility will serve as one of the keys to the success of G•R•O•W.

Involving Youth in G•R•O•W

Youth will generally get more excited about participating in G•R•O•W if they all visit on the same night each month rather than assigning them throughout the month. In theory it would seem more effective for youth to participate each week, but youth will be more

> **The report time allows them to hear other reports of visits that have gone well.**

motivated to attend when the entire group is present. It is also easier for the youth minister to organize one outreach event per month. Sunday School teachers in the youth department should be asked to commit to the youth G•R•O•W night. This makes transportation for youth visits much more practical.

Providing Child Care

If you want young couples involved in the G•R•O•W outreach program, you will need to provide child care. This can be accomplished in two ways. First, if finances permit, paid child care workers may be provided for children. Second, some members may feel their commitment to G•R•O•W is child care on one G•R•O•W night per month. Their ministry is just as legitimate as those making visits, writing letters, or making calls.

Setting Up the G•R•O•W Room

The G•R•O•W room is critical to the success of the program. A designated area of the church for G•R•O•W should be provided and must not be changed! The room, even if used for other purposes, should cause people to think outreach whether they are in the room for Bible study or outreach during the week. A frequent change of location for G•R•O•W will communicate that outreach is less than a priority. Maps and promotional materials should be permanent fixtures in the G•R•O•W room. (See illustration 15, Outreach Ministry G•R•O•W Night, in the appendix.)

A good time for the G•R•O•W banquet is at the beginning or end of the training each year.

Reporting the Visits

The report time is one of the most important aspects of the G•R•O•W night. Not every person will have a great visitation experience every G•R•O•W night. The report time allows them to hear other reports of visits that have gone well.

Leaders should remind participants that most of the contacts made on outreach night are cultivation contacts. No contact should be viewed as unsuccessful. Frequent updates on conversions and additions to the church that have resulted from these cultivation contacts will encourage participants that the harvest always belongs to God and not to the laborers.

Planning a G•R•O•W Banquet

Each year we plan a G•R•O•W banquet where we provide a meal and brief program for all those who have participated in G•R•O•W the previous year. Potential G•R•O•W participants are also invited, but the banquet is churchwide. The event serves as a reward and celebration for those who have worked in the G•R•O•W program. Testimonies from participants as well as those who have made decisions for Christ as a result of the G•R•O•W ministry are shared. A good time for the G•R•O•W banquet is at the beginning or end of the training each year.

These are just a few areas of review that might make the implementation of the G•R•O•W program a bit easier. Review the implementation schedule so that important elements aren't overlooked.

---

[1] Thom Rainer, *Effective Evangelistic Churches* (Nashville: Broadman & Holman Publishers, 1996), 13.

Chapter 14

Keeping the Ball Rolling

How we finish the Christian walk is much more important than how we start. Many church programs and ministries start with a boom and slowly begin to die. One of the most important characteristics of the G•R•O•W outreach program is that momentum can be sustained and should even increase over time. One of the reasons for increased momentum and enthusiasm is that the success of the ministry becomes more and more evident with time.

The outreach and evangelism program of any church should be the top objective and strategy toward fulfilling its mission statement and the Great Commission. This priority should be reflected as each staff member participates and promotes the G•R•O•W outreach program.

The G•R•O•W outreach ministry can serve as an effective tool in each ministry of the fellowship. For example, when the music ministry of West Jackson Baptist Church presents special events at Christmas and Easter, guest information is carefully recorded; and letters are written to guests on subsequent outreach nights. When Octoberfest, our alternative to the celebration of Halloween, occurs as an outreach to the children of our church and community, guests and their unchurched families are cultivated through the G•R•O•W outreach ministry.

These team members are special, and we want the whole church to know it!

This chapter deals with three important elements of keeping the ball rolling.

Commissioning the Teams

A consistent promotion of the outreach ministry through a weekly mailout or Sunday order of service is helpful, but no method has proved more effective than conducting a brief commissioning of the current week's outreach team during the morning worship service. At the conclusion of each morning worship service, we ask all the members of the team that will meet the following Tuesday to stand. Then we ask our fellowship to pray specifically for these people the following week.

This brief time accomplishes a couple of things. First, if the members of the outreach team stand and are recognized publicly, they feel more compelled to be present for outreach. Second, commissioning the teams during the morning service on a weekly basis instills the importance of outreach in the minds of the fellowship at large. These team members are special, and we want the whole church to know it!

Ongoing Recruitment

Ongoing recruitment is one of the basic responsibilities of team captains. They will be more effective at this than the pastor and staff. During the year, they are encouraged to recruit new church members and long-term church members who are not a part of G•R•O•W.

But this level of ongoing recruitment is not enough to get all members involved. At the end of each church year, we compile a list of all new church members who have not yet joined a G•R•O•W

> **Obviously a program geared for growth will create certain obstacles.**

team. Many may not fully realize just what G•R•O•W is all about.

This list is divided up evenly among the team captains. They are asked to contact each person personally about being on a G•R•O•W team. Once they are recruited, they are asked to participate in the annual G•R•O•W training conducted in January.

Presently at West Jackson, all members of the G•R•O•W program are asked to go through the training every other year. During the weeks of recruitment, we use G•R•O•W testimonies of those who have come to Christ or the church through the G•R•O•W ministry. This serves as a powerful motivation for people to become involved in the ministry. After all, they are hearing firsthand accounts that G•R•O•W works!

Overcoming Obstacles to G•R•O•W

Obviously a program geared for growth will create certain obstacles. The ability of the pastor to help his church adjust to growth is just as important as the program that helps generate that growth. Here are some of the more pronounced obstacles I have encountered during the implementation of the G•R•O•W outreach program.

G•R•O•W night conflicts.—As the G•R•O•W program begins, making the G•R•O•W night a priority in programming will not be difficult. But as times goes on, it becomes more and more critical to keep other events off the designated night of G•R•O•W outreach. If exceptions are made, then more exceptions will be requested. That is why it will be imperative to make the time of G•R•O•W the only event that happens in your church during that time.

We do not allow church-sponsored sporting events to be scheduled during this time. Committee meetings should not be scheduled during the designated outreach time. A challenge to this designated time priority will occur most from those who are not a part of the G•R•O•W program. The pastor may find it necessary to have other leadership groups in the church to affirm this commitment. A lack of priority to the G•R•O•W outreach night will translate into a lack of priority to the mission of reaching one's city for Christ.

Other churches' response to G•R•O•W.—Since this program of outreach is aggressive as well as successful, the pastor may find that his church undergoes some level of scrutiny from other churches. Growing churches are not always well liked by other churches in the community that are not growing. Such an aggressive approach to outreach might be perceived as a threat to those churches.

One way to offset that potential obstacle is to affirm publicly other churches and state that the objective of the G•R•O•W program is not to reach the churched but the unchurched. Another way we counter this problem is by not having our ministerial staff to visit guests who are members of other local churches unless they have been personally requested to do so.

Increased workload for staff.—Preparing the assignments for one night of G•R•O•W can take as much as eight hours for one ministerial staff member. Depending on the initial number of participants and the size of the prospect file, it may require the addition of a part-time secretary to handle the additional clerical work. After the G•R•O•W outreach night, some time is necessary to log in and update the results for the prospect file. The pastor should plan for and expect an increase in his workload. A smaller church may be able to use some volunteer office help for this task.

Development of a "church marketing" mentality.—I must constantly remind our congregation that we are marketing Jesus and not our

Soul-winning should remain the primary objective of each G•R•O•W night of outreach.

church. One of the most promising results of the G•R•O•W program is that members become more excited about the future of the church. An ungodly pride could develop as people see their efforts resulting in growth. That is the reason soul-winning should remain the primary objective of each G•R•O•W night of outreach.

Assimilation of new members.—The pastor should not begin the G•R•O•W program unless he expects growth. He should not expect growth unless he makes plans for growth. A plan for an increase in the number of Bible study classes should be in place. The discipleship ministry should also include provisions for new Christian and new member classes. The church should be prepared for new people who want to serve. Failure to provide avenues for service will result in new members becoming inactive or choosing to serve in other churches. A well-conceived plan for the assimilation of new members will make this obstacle much less of a problem for the pastor and church.

Making Growth a Reality

No outreach program will generate a mind-set of growth in the local church. But once the pastor and congregation develop a desire for growth and reaching people for Christ, the G•R•O•W outreach program will serve as a wonderful tool to make the vision for growth a reality. The G•R•O•W outreach program works because it is biblically based, people friendly, applicable to any church, and Christ centered. May your church be blessed with "teams that win" through the G•R•O•W outreach ministry!

Appendix

Illustration 1

Prospect Search Card

G•R•O•W PROSPECT SEARCH

THE PERSON LISTED BELOW IS A PROSPECT
FOR WEST JACKSON BAPTIST CHURCH

Name _____

Address _____

Approximate Age _____   Phone _____

- ❏ Not a Christian
- ❏ Baptist (elsewhere)
- ❏ Has Visited WJBC

- ❏ Family Attends Our Church
- ❏ Family Unchurched
- ❏ Newcomer to Jackson

Other comments _____

_____

_____

Your Name _____

Phone_____

Illustration 2

Sunday Worship Registration Card

Welcome to
West Jackson Baptist Church
November 2, 1997
Hour of Worship
❏ 8:30 a.m. ❏ 10:50 a.m. ❏ 6:00 p.m.

Mr./Ms./Mrs. _____
Address _____
Apt. Name _____ Apt. # _____
City _____
State _____ Zip _____
Home Phone _____
Work Phone _____
Birth date: Month ____Day ____Year ____
Children/Ages _____

❏ Married ❏ Single ❏ Student
Grade ___

Current Church Membership:
❏ West Jackson Baptist
Another Church:
❏ **Local** ❏ **Out of Town**
Name_____
City _____
Guest:
❏ First Time ❏ Second Time
❏ Regular Attender
I'd like more information on:
❏ How to become a Christian
❏ How to join this church
❏ Sunday morning Bible study
❏ Music ministries
❏ Recreation ministries
❏ Senior-adult ministries
❏ Singles ministries/college ministries
❏ Youth ministries
❏ Children's ministries (grades 1 - 6)
❏ Preschool ministries (birth - 5 years)

I would like you to know that:
❏ I'm considering committing my life
to Christ.
❏ I want to be baptized.
❏ I want to join this church.
❏ I'd like to talk to a pastor.
❏ I want to enroll in a Sunday morning
Bible study.
❏ Other_____

_____

_____

_____

How did you learn of our church?
❏ Newspaper
❏ Yellow pages
❏ Friend_____
❏ Mail
❏ TV/Radio
❏ Other_____

Other Requests
❏ Prayer request
❏ Communication to church staff

_____

_____

_____

_____

_____

Illustration 3

Special Events Registration Card

The Sounds of Christmas

West Jackson Baptist Church
Jackson, Tennessee

❑ Friday, December 12   ❑ Saturday, December 13   ❑ Sunday, December 14

Mr./Ms./Mrs. _____ Home Phone _____

Address _____ Work Phone _____

Apt. Name _____ Apt. # _____

City _____ State _____ Zip_____

Birth date: Month _____ Day _____ Year _____

Children/Ages_____ _____ _____ _____- _____

❑ Married   ❑ Single   ❑ Student – Grade _____

Current Church Membership: ❑ West Jackson Baptist Church
❑ Another Church: ❑ Local ❑ Out of Town

Church _____ City _____

GUEST: ❑ First Time   ❑ Second Time   ❑ Regular Attender

I would like to make the following decision tonight:

❑ I want to be baptized.   ❑ I am committing my life to Jesus Christ.

❑ I want to join this church.   ❑ I am recommitting my life to Jesus Christ.

❑ I would like to talk to a pastor.   ❑ I want to enroll in Sunday morning Bible study.

❑ Other: _____

I would like more information on:

❑ How to become a Christian ❑ How to join this church ❑ Sunday morning Bible study

❑ Music ministries ❑ Recreation ministries ❑ Senior-adult ministries

❑ Single-adult ministries ❑ College ministries ❑ Youth ministries

❑ Children's ministries (grades 1 - 6) ❑ Preschool ministries (birth - 5 yrs.)

Other Requests:

Prayer requests: _____ Communication to church staff: _____

_____ _____

_____ _____

_____ _____

Illustration 4

G•R•O•W
Team Captains

4 Areas of Responsibility

1. Recruitment.—Captains are responsible for recruiting team members. People who enroll as team members will commit to participate one Tuesday night a month. If they are unable to participate on their designated team night, they should be encouraged to make it up another Tuesday night.

2. Attendance.—Captains are responsible for attending G•R•O•W and seeing that team members receive a monthly reminder to encourage attendance. Team members will be dropped from team rosters if they miss participating in G•R•O•W for three months in a row.

3. G•R•O•W night.—Captains are responsible for assisting the pastor and staff on their designated G•R•O•W night. Assistance will be required with the following:

> (EARLY ARRIVAL NEEDED ☞ 6:40 P.M.)
> 1. Welcoming
> 2. Visitation and phone-call assignments
> 3. Letter-writing assignments
> 4. Refreshments

4. Meetings.—Captains will be responsible for attending G•R•O•W captains meetings on an as-needed basis.

Illustration 5

Enrollment Card

GOD REWARDS OUR WORK

G•R•O•W Outreach Ministry

Name _____

Address _____

Phone _____

❏ Yes, I will commit to participate *once a month* in G•R•O•W.

I prefer to participate:
❏ 1st Tuesday, G Team
❏ 2nd Tuesday, R Team
❏ 3rd Tuesday, O Team
❏ 4th Tuesday, W Team

❏ I am willing to serve on any Tuesday!

❏ I cannot commit to participate at this time.

Illustration 6

G•R•O•W Sample Letter 1:
VISITORS/PROSPECTS

(Date)

Dear _____,

Thank you for visiting with us at West Jackson Baptist Church. We hope you felt "at home" and that you experienced the presence of the Lord. We believe God has commissioned our fellowship to touch the hearts of the people in Jackson with His love.

We want to invite you to visit one of our Bible study classes on Sunday morning at 9:30. We have classes for everyone, and each class is led by a teacher who loves and cares for each member.

If we can help you in any way, please let us know. We hope to see you again soon.

Sincerely,

(Sign your name.)

Special Instructions
Include brochure with this letter.
Also, please enclose any information that visitors/prospects have requested on Guest Registration *form and that is available at G•R•O•W.*

Illustration 7

G•R•O•W Sample Letter 2:
VISITORS—
ACTIVE IN ANOTHER CHURCH

(Date)

Dear _____,

Thank you for visiting with us at West Jackson Baptist Church. We hope you felt "at home" and that you experienced the presence of the Lord. We believe God has commissioned our fellowship to touch the hearts of the people in Jackson with His love.

Please feel free to worship with us anytime you have the opportunity. If we can help you in any way, please let us know.

Sincerely,

(Sign your name.)

Special Instructions
<u>**Do not**</u> **include brochure with this letter.**

Illustration 8

G•R•O•W Sample Letter 3:
VISITORS—OUT OF TOWN

(Date)

Dear _____,

Thank you for visiting with us this past Sunday at West Jackson Baptist Church. We hope you felt "at home" and that you experienced the presence of the Lord. We believe God has commissioned our fellowship to touch the hearts of the people in Jackson with His love.

If we can help you in any way, please let us know. We hope you will visit us again when you are in Jackson.

Sincerely,

(Sign your name.)

Special Instructions
Do not include brochure with this letter.

Illustration 9

G•R•O•W Sample Letter 4:
NEWCOMERS

(Date)

Dear _____,

We know you are probably still very busy getting settled in your new residence. Since you have either just moved to the Jackson area or made a move within the region, we would consider it an honor if you would visit West Jackson Baptist Church and worship with us. We are located at the corner of Campbell and Deaderick Streets.

West Jackson is a place where people feel at home immediately. It would be a wonderful place for you to meet new friends and strengthen your relationship with God.

We hope to see you soon.

Sincerely,

(Sign your name.)

Special Instructions
Include brochure with this letter.

Illustration 10

G•R•O•W Sample Letter 5:
POSSIBLE NEWCOMERS

(Date)

Dear _____,

It has come to our attention that you are considering a possible move to Jackson, Tennessee. We would like to take this opportunity to welcome you to our city and invite you to visit our church. West Jackson Baptist Church is a Christ-centered, warm, and friendly fellowship. We strive to meet the needs of each family member by providing Bible study and activities for all age groups.

If and when you get to Jackson, we hope you and your family will call us if we can be of any assistance in any way.

Sincerely,

(Sign your name.)

Special Instructions
Include brochure with this letter.

Illustration 11

G•R•O•W Sample Letter 6:
VISITING AGAIN—PROSPECTS

(Date)

Dear _____,

Thank you so much for visiting us again at West Jackson Baptist Church. We just want you to know that we will continue to pray with you as you seek the Lord's will concerning a church home.

If we can help you in any way, please let us know. The church office number is (901) 424-1800. Again, thank you for your continued interest in our fellowship.

Sincerely,

(Sign your name.)
. . . . Option 2· . . . .

We just want you to know that we continue to pray with you as you seek God's leadership concerning a church home. We hope you will continue to worship with us as often as possible. You are also invited to attend any or all activities here at West Jackson.

Again, thank you so much for visiting our fellowship. If we can do anything for you or your family, please let us know.

Special Instructions
Do not enclose a WJBC brochure with either letter. Do enclose any infor-mation they have requested and is available at G•R•O•W. Please use Option 2 letter for those indicating they are "regular attenders" on guest registration form.

Illustration 12

G•R•O•W Sample Letter 7: SYMPATHY

(Date)

Dear _____,

We at West Jackson Baptist Church express to you our deepest sympathy upon the recent loss of your loved one. We are praying for you and your family. If we can help you in any way, please feel free to call our church at 424-1800.

May God bless you, and may His Holy Spirit comfort you at this time.

In Christ's love,

(Sign your name.)

Special Instructions
This is only a sample letter; please feel free to add your own words of sympathy and encouragement. <u>Do not</u> enclose a church brochure.

Illustration 13

G·R·O·W
Sign-in/Roster

G TEAM

MEMBERS' NAMES	OCTOBER	NOVEMBER	DECEMBER
Curlin, Betty	A	L	V
Curlin, Harvey Lee	V	X	V
Davis, Carolyn	L	L	L
Davis, Ron	L	T	T
Depriest, Bobby	X	T	V
Deschenes, Diane	V	X	A
Deschenes, Paul	V	L	V

Place *one* of the following letters in the current month column
to indicate attendance and area of involvement:
V (visiting), **T** (telephone calling), **L** (letter writing), **A** (anywhere), or **X** (absent)

Illustration 14

G•R•O•W Visitation Assignment Sheet

West Jackson Baptist Church Prospect

Date Last Update 11/4/97

04094-01	Burks, Tom	(H) 901-456-7890
VISIT AREA	1234 Main St.	(P)
SEC #24	Jackson, TN 38305-1357	(W) 901-234-4567

GENDER M   MARITAL STATUS M   SPECIAL CODE 060897

SOURCE A   RELATIONSHIP   DATE INPUT   10/05/97

AGE   40   BIRTH DATE   02/22/57   MAIL CODE

SPECIAL COMMENT: wife–Pam

MEMBER OF: Grace Baptist, Boaz, AR

DATES VISITED CHURCH: 10/05/97   10/12/97   10/19/97

COMMENTS:

10/06/97	COMMEN	Tom and Pam visited 10:50 a.m. worship and Sunday School Adult B Coed 3 class. They have recently moved to Jackson and are looking for a church home. Indicated they "would like to talk with pastor" on guest registration card./ls
10/07/97	COMMEN	Pastor had a good visit with Tom and Pam. Recommends a follow-up visit by a couple./ls
10/14/97	COMMEN	Letter written by G Team on 10/14/97./ls

Illustration 15

Outreach Ministry G•R•O•W Night

Captains are responsible for assisting pastor and staff on their designated G•R•O•W night. Assistance will be required with the following:

1. Welcoming
2. Visitation and phone-call assignments
3. Letter-writing assignments
4. Refreshments

(EARLY ARRIVAL NEEDED ☞ 6:40 P.M.)

AREA 1 – WELCOMING
o Greeting
o Signing In
o Name Tags
o Directing

AREA 2 – VISITATION AND PHONE-CALL ASSIGNMENTS
o See that people who are making visits get signed in with partner (try to pair up people).
o Take assignments or give assignments to visiting teams.
o Check sign-in to see if any "A" people are needed to assist with visiting.
o Any assignments not taken should be assigned to phone callers.
o Be sure returning teams get signed in on "Report Order" board.
o Be responsible for tallying contacts as visits are reported.
o Any visiting team that comes in after report time has begun will need to be put on "Report Order."
o Receive completed assignments, being sure some notation or comment is recorded about contact.

Illustration 15
(cont.)

o Place completed assignments in "completed assignment file."
o Receive phone assignments. Find out how many contacts were made, either number of households contacted x 2 or the number of people in each household contacted (if known).
o Find out if any calls need particular attention.

AREA 3 – LETTER-WRITING ASSIGNMENTS
o Table set up: See that each table is properly arranged. Involve early comers. (Be sure to set up a model table to go by.)
o Begin handing out writing assignments by 6:50 p.m. if several team members are present.
o Be available to answer questions to the best of your ability.
o About every 10-15 minutes make a pass through letter writers, collecting all completed assignments and form letters.
o Look over assignments to be sure some notation is made indicating assignment was complete, i.e., initials, date, check mark, just about any marking will be sufficient.
o Separate and file completed assignment in "completed assignment folder" and file form letters in numerically coded pending files.
o Begin final collection at 7:55 p.m.
o Replace letter-writing materials in green pocket folders. (No specific order is necessary.) Please be sure *no* writing assignments or form letters are mistakenly put in the pocket folders.
o Return pocket folders to plastic mail crate.

AREA 4 – REFRESHMENTS
o Provide a refreshment sign-up sheet.
o Call members who have signed up to remind them to bring refreshments on their assigned night.
o Be sure coffee, cold drinks, and other items are arranged for members to serve themselves.

Calendar

14-Week Calendar
Implementing the G•R•O•W Outreach Program

WEEK 1
- Begin preaching series on biblical evangelism and outreach (chapter 6).
- Start creating and organizing prospect file (chapter 7).
- Start enlisting team captains (chapter 8).

WEEK 2
- Continue preaching series (chapter 6).
- Continue creating and organizing prospect file (chapter 7).
- Continue enlisting team captains (chapter 8).

WEEK 3
- Continue preaching series (chapter 6).
- Continue creating and organizing prospect file (chapter 7).
- Complete selection of team captains (chapter 8).
- Start conducting an "in-house" prospect search (chapter 7).

WEEK 4
- Complete preaching series (chapter 6).
- Continue creating and organizing prospect file (chapter 7).
- Continue in-house prospect search (chapter 7).
- Conduct training for team captains (chapter 8).

> **One of the most fruitful methods of assimilating prospects is through an in-house prospect search.**

- Begin developing outreach materials—brochures, witnessing tracts, forms, etc. (chapter 13).

WEEK 5
- Continue creating and organizing prospect file (chapter 7).
- Continue in-house prospect search (chapter 7).
- Begin enlisting team members (chapter 8).
- Set target date for first outreach night (chapter 13).
- Continue developing outreach materials (chapter 13).

WEEK 6
- Continue organizing prospect file (chapter 7).
- Continue in-house prospect search (chapter 7).
- Continue enlisting team members (chapter 8).
- Continue developing outreach materials (chapter 13).

WEEK 7
- Continue organizing prospect file (chapter 7).
- Continue in-house prospect search (chapter 7).
- Continue enlisting team members (chapter 8).
- Continue developing outreach materials (chapter 13).
- Organize material needed for training team members (chapter 9).

WEEK 8
- Continue organizing prospect file (chapter 7).
- Continue in-house prospect search (chapter 7).
- Meet with captains to balance the team lists (chapter 8).
- Complete developing outreach materials (chapter 13).
- Set up room for G•R•O•W training (chapter 13).

> **The report time allows them to hear other reports of visits that have gone well.**

WEEK 9
- Continue organizing prospect file (chapter 7).
- Continue in-house prospect search (chapter 7).
- Begin G•R•O•W training (chapters 9-12).
- Collect lists and materials needed for letter writing (chapter 13).

WEEK 10
- Continue organizing prospect file (chapter 7).
- Continue in-house prospect search (chapter 7).
- Continue G•R•O•W training (chapter 9).
- Continue collecting materials needed for letter writing (chapter 13).

WEEK 11
- Continue organizing prospect file (chapter 7).
- Continue in-house prospect search (chapter 7).
- Continue G•R•O•W training (chapter 9-12).
- Continue collecting lists and materials needed for letter writing (chapter 13).
- Begin setup of "outreach center" or "outreach headquarters" (chapter 13).

WEEK 12
- Continue organizing prospect file (chapter 7).
- Close out in-house prospect search (chapter 7).
- Complete G•R•O•W training (chapter 9–12).
- Finish setup of outreach center or outreach headquarters (chapter 13).
- Begin selecting prospects to be contacted on first night of outreach (chapter 13).
- Set up "welcome centers" around the church (chapter 13).

Participants, like the first disciples, need the fellowship of another laborer.

WEEK 13
- High attendance day on Sunday (chapter 13).

WEEK 14
- First night of G•R•O•W following high attendance day on Sunday (chapters 13-14).

Notes

Notes

....
....
....
....
....
....
....
....
....
....
....
....
....
....

Notes

....

....

....

....

....

....

....

....

....

....

....

....

....

....

....

Notes

....
....
....
....
....
....
....
....
....
....
....
....
....
....
....
....

Notes

....

....

....

....

....

....

....

....

....

....

....

....

....

....

....

....

Notes

....
....
....
....
....
....
....
....
....
....
....
....
....
....
....